# A MOTHER'S STORY

# Mary Beth Whitehead
# A Mother's Story

### The Truth About the Baby M Case

## with
## Loretta
## Schwartz-Nobel

ST. MARTIN'S PRESS
NEW YORK

Design by Glen M. Edelstein

Library of Congress Cataloging-in-Publication Data

Whitehead, Mary Beth.
    A mother's story.

    1. Whitehead, Mary Beth.    2. Surrogate mothers—
New Jersey—Biography.    I. Schwartz-Nobel, Loretta.
II. Title.
HQ759.5.W48   1989        306.8'743'0924        88-29892
ISBN 0-312-02614-5

First Edition
10 9 8 7 6 5 4 3 2 1

For Melissa, Ryan, and Tuesday; and for all the other children born of surrogate arrangements, and their brothers and sisters, in the hope that they will not suffer as my children did.

# Contents

**Contents**

# Acknowledgments

So many people offered me friendship and support that it is difficult to name them all. First, I'd like to thank a group of women who took the time and effort to organize themselves on my behalf: Rosemary Bailey, Jacqueline Donatuccio, Jean Grasso, Angela Hanlon, Viola Hannon, Rena Kamena, Kathleen Karvak, Barbara Lakick, Maureen Larsen, Henryka Laskowski, Francesca McPhee, Julia Nock, Kathy Rutler, and Joan Wiley. They are truly as their name suggests, Mothers With Feelings. Second, I would like to thank a group of men who organized the New Jersey Citizens Against Surrogate Parenting: Arthur Bodenheim, David Donatuccio, Richard Kruse, Matthew Laskowski, and Jim Nock.

Next, I'd like to thank both new and old friends for their tireless efforts on my behalf: Camille and Frank Agovino, Barbara and Chuck Anderson, Anita Andrus, Joan Badkock, Judy and Jeff Benson, Phyllis Chesler, Patty Clayton, Gena Corea, Linda Couch, Sharon DeAngelo-Huddle, Rich and Irene Devine, Irene and Tim Foley, Betty Fornaro, Laurie and Steve Garda, Rosemary Gross, CiCi Harrison, Heather Harrison, Michele Harrison, Sue Hergenhan, Ellen and John Hochberg, Kathy Iseman, Mary Teresa and Steve Jeffies, Elizabeth and Tim Karcher, Cathy Koller, Linda Meserol, Abby Michaels, Jenny Michaels, Joel Nobel, Betty Ann Pacilli, Lucy Pacilli, Rochelle and Mark Picchierri, Annie Rajoppi, Fay Rosenberg, Mr. and Mrs. Saleino, Sharon Simmons, Maria Ventresco, Alison Ward, and Debbie Yetka. While their individual contributions are too numerous to list here, each of them remembers what they have done for me and I will never forget.

I'd also like to thank Nancy Soloman, June Whitehead, Bobbie Whitehead, Edward Whitehead, and Irene Kulver for their support and guidance.

I can never adequately express my love and appreciation to the members of my own family: Andrea Rockhill; Jules, Kevin, Michael, and Karen Erbe; and especially my mother and father, Eileen and Joseph Messer, my brothers, Donnie and Jeff, and my sister-in-law, Sherri. Their warmth and kindness made even the worst days bearable.

The Coalition Against Surrogacy founders Jeremy Rifkin, Andrew Kimbrell, and Matt Powell opened a whole new world to me, as did the surrogate mothers I came to know: Nancy Barrass, Patty Foster, Mary Beth Simmelink, and Laurie Yates.

I am also grateful to Dr. Joseph Marino and the nurses who assisted him, and to Dr. Thomas Gianis, Dr. Jeffrey Glickman, Dr. Donald Klein, Dr. Harold Koplewicz, Dr. Steven Nickman, Dr. Phyllis Silverman, and Dr. Bert Sokoloff.

I'd like to express my love and gratitude to my husband, Dean Gould, his parents, Mildred and Arthur Gould, and his brothers, Craig and Todd, as well as Anthony Affatali, Raymond Vino, and the firm of Spicer and Oppenheim.

Nor can I ever adequately thank Harold Cassidy and his wife, Randee; Roger Foss; Heidi Hellring; Randy Wolf; Bob Ruggieri; Mary Ellen Edwards; Phil SanFilippo; Robin Gavin; Virginia Flynn; Alan and Peggy Karcher; Lou Rainone and his wife, Mary; Emily Alman and her husband,

David; Robert Arenstein and his wife, Judy; Alan M. Grosman and his wife, Betty; and Joel D. Siegal and his wife, Ronnie.

I want to thank Claudia Disu for typing endless drafts of this manuscript, and my literary agents, Elliot Hoffman and Myron Beldock, and Ellen Levine and her assistant, Diana Finch, for efforts that went way beyond the call of duty. I could not have completed this project without the help of my fine editor, Roy Gainsburg.

I am also grateful to many members of the media for their kindness. And the Bergen County Sheriff's officers for help that went beyond their assigned jobs.

I'd also like to thank all the people who sent gifts and letters of support, signed petitions, and offered friendship. Your collective spirits saw me through the darkest moments.

Last but most important, Rick, Tuesday, Ryan, Melissa, I can never thank you enough for giving me the strength to carry on.

Mary Beth Whitehead

# An Opening Explanation

Wherever I go, people seem to know who I am. Sometimes they turn and whisper, "There's Mary Beth Whitehead." A few are hostile. Many approach me with tears in their eyes. Occasionally they give me advice. They almost always ask questions.

For a long time I have been silent. When scores of reporters camped out on my lawn for days at a time or blocked my path with microphones and asked countless questions, I usually did not respond. I have repeatedly turned down interview requests from Barbara Walters, Phil Donahue, and dozens of others. Even when other people involved in the case have attacked me on network television, I have remained silent.

There were moments when the public humiliation and personal pain were so great that I thought of giving up. But the joy of Sara's smile when we were together, as cellmates, for two hours once a week, and her tears as she was lifted from my arms by guards who said that "your time is up," always renewed my determination. Even the most restrictive, prisonlike setting could not destroy our bond or change the fact that she was still my daughter. There could never be a court-ordered termination of our love. For her sake, I always found the strength to carry on.

For those of you who ask why I call her Sara in this book and in the courtroom, I must explain that when she was born and during the litigation, Sara Whitehead was her legal name. Now she lives with the Sterns and they call her Melissa. It was very difficult for me to give up the name Sara, but in order to avoid confusing her, I, too, have begun to call her Melissa.

So many people have speculated about why I am finally breaking my silence and writing a book that I've decided to start by explaining my reasons. I did not write this book to become well known. The newspaper accounts, magazine articles, and television shows have already brought me far more public attention than I ever cared to have.

I did not write this book to make a lot of money. Money has *never* been important to me. If it were, I would not have married the man I married at sixteen and remained his wife for so many years. Money is not important to me now, except to have enough to pay back the people who have so generously helped me in the fight for my daughter.

Nor did I write this book to hurt the Sterns. If I had wanted to do that, I could have launched personal attacks and made them public, just as the Sterns did. I would have found the skeletons that exist in *every* family's closet. Even when Betsy Stern made real her threat to drag me through the mud in court, I did not respond by doing the same. I felt that in the long run that would only hurt my daughter.

I didn't even write this book because I oppose surrogate parenting, although I do now. I have learned in the most painful way that the rental of a woman's body and the sale of the child she bears is wrong. It violates the core of what a woman is. I have also learned that older children can never believe and trust a mother who tells them that they are loved and valued and that it's only their baby brother or sister who had a price tag.

I did not attempt to write the definitive work on the "new" problem of surrogacy. From my perspective, surrogacy isn't even new. It's been going on as long as there have been women and poor women, ever since Abraham had Hagar the slave bear his child. This newly publicized right to buy and sell human beings or to rent parts of them does not represent a brave new technological beginning. It represents a step backward into the worst traditions of our past.

I have learned all of these things the hard way, and although I deeply hope that other women will learn from my mistakes, I am not a public crusader. I am simply a mother and housewife who has decided it is time to set the record straight.

I have written this book because there have been a great many misconceptions about what really happened and why I did what I did. From the start, the public was exposed to highly selective and biased information. Very few of the facts about the contract that I signed, the Infertility Center, the Sterns, the lower-court judge, the court-appointed guardian, or the police have ever been revealed. Perhaps I could have continued to live with my own pain at being misunderstood and misjudged, but the suffering that my family has been forced to endure is more than I can accept.

I wrote this book because it is time that all of the facts were made public. For my children, for my friends, for the many thousands of people who have supported me, and most of all for my daughter. It is time, past time, to tell this story the way it really happened, so that someday, when she is old enough, Melissa will understand the truth about her mother, my weaknesses and my strengths, the terrible mistake that I made, and how very much I love her.

MARY BETH WHITEHEAD

# A Note About the Collaboration

I first wrote to Mary Beth Whitehead in March of 1987. We met at a restaurant in Hackensack, New Jersey, a few days later.

I remember watching her walk through the crowd with her head lowered so that she wouldn't be recognized. When I introduced myself, she looked up and held out her hand. I was amazed at how much younger, softer, and prettier she was than she had appeared in most of her photographs.

I, like millions of other Americans, had been following the daily struggle for Baby M through press accounts and media coverage. For most of the preceding month, I had been on a promotion tour for my most recently published book. But no matter what city I was in or how tired I was, I never went to sleep without checking the newspapers to see what had happened in the Baby M case that day.

Like Mary Beth, I had recently had a baby. I, too, had married as a teenager, had two older children, and had never anticipated wanting a third child. As a mother, I felt deeply connected with her fierce love for her baby, and her struggle against all odds to keep the child.

I could also identify with Bill Stern, however. Like Bill, I had recently lost a parent. I knew what it was to long for a child, partly as a legacy and biological link to a dearly loved dead father. I, too, was married to a physician. In short, I was a journalist who initially had sympathy and a sense of connection with both Mary Beth Whitehead and Bill Stern. I approached this story as I had approached many others. I did not start out with a bias. I had won more than a dozen national awards for independent investigative magazine reporting, had written two nonfiction books, and had turned down several offers for collaborations, precisely because I was not willing to compromise my journalistic integrity.

But the more I explored the facts as an objective reporter, the more firmly I came to believe that the *real* story of the Baby M case had never been told. In fact, it had been hidden. A bias against Mary Beth had permeated the press, the news media, and almost every other aspect of our collective thinking. Otherwise thoughtful people appeared to have followed the herd without regard for fact or reason. One psychiatrist I knew actually asked if Mary Beth still believed that she was *really* the baby's mother. An English professor proudly announced that she hated Mary Beth, then reluctantly admitted that she didn't know why. Suddenly, people who wouldn't have thought twice about someone else breaking a business or even a marriage contract rigidly insisted that Mary Beth Whitehead be held to hers. Yet virtually no one questioned a judge who sent half a dozen armed policemen to separate a nursing baby from her perfectly fit mother. No one questioned a father who obtained an invalid paternity order from an unqualified judge. No one asked if the contract was illegal or if a man's sperm and his money were really worth more than a mother's love. Surprisingly few people asked if it was right or even legal to use contract and penal law to forever separate this infant from her mother.

With Judge Harvey Sorkow's termination of Mary Beth's parental rights and his devastating assault on her character from the bench, the cultural phenomenon seemed all but complete. Mary Beth Whitehead had become a national scapegoat.

I was reminded of Shirley Jackson's horror story, "The Lottery," an allegory in which one member of an otherwise unremarkable community is stoned to death for no apparent reason.

Two days after Judge Sorkow's ruling, I set out for Bricktown, New Jersey, with my eight-month-old baby and my seventy-nine-year-old mother. I rented an apartment near Mary Beth's house and began to work with her to tell her story.

Mary Beth spoke and I listened. Often we waited until the children were asleep to talk about the most painful parts, then worked late into the night. Together we recorded the details of her struggle, her determination, and her anguish.

During the months since our first meeting in Hackensack, I came to know a woman who was trusting, generous, and forgiving to a fault. I do believe that, despite all that has happened, if the Sterns were willing, Mary Beth would embrace them tomorrow. As the syndicated columnist Murray Kempton put it, "For all vagaries she is of stuff heroic, and that is too seldom available for the viewing."

Long before the Supreme Court of New Jersey confirmed my view, I was convinced that justice had not been rendered in the Baby M case. Fortunately and wisely, that court has forever altered the outcome of this struggle, the future of surrogacy in the United States, and the public perception of Mary Beth Whitehead.

In ruling that the contract was illegal, that surrogacy is indeed "the sale of a child," and that Mary Beth White-head is both the biological and the legal mother of Melissa Stern, the New Jersey Supreme Court has also granted her a permanent place in history and the stature she deserves. Surely, if not for her loss, her courage, and her tenacity, that which is now illegal and a crime punishable by imprisonment in several states would have endured, per-haps indefinitely. Countless thousands of infants would have been bought before they were conceived, sold at birth, and forcibly separated forever from their mothers, in a country that prides itself on freedom.

LORETTA SCHWARTZ-NOBEL

# Chapter 1

# Giving Birth

Sarah suggested that Abraham impregnate Hagar in order "that I may obtain children by her," but Hagar was a slave. What's modern about this story is that once pregnant, Hagar, like Mary Beth Whitehead, seemed to think that her child was hers, no matter what anyone said. . . .

—Katha Pollitt in *The Nation*,
May 23, 1987

**T**he day of Sara's birth, March 27, 1986, was the day it all became real. At first the pains were not intense. Just a backache that I'd had all night. But it was a timed backache, so after I sent my daughter to school I drove to the hospital. They put me in a labor room and hooked me up to a fetal monitor. When the doctor came into the examining room to check me, he said he'd break my water and put me back on the monitor.

I remember asking the nurse if she could get me dry sheets. Then the pain came: devastating, unbelievable pain. The baby was right there; she was ready to be born. Then, just as suddenly, everything stopped. For about ten minutes I had no contractions, no pain, nothing. It was as if I weren't in labor anymore, as if I weren't even pregnant. The doctor left the room saying we'd be there all day because I wasn't concentrating hard enough.

Actually, I was concentrating harder than he could imagine. "I can't do it," I thought. "I just can't deliver this child." Underneath, I think a part of me already knew that I wouldn't be able to give her up, and everything in me was trying to hold on to her as long as I could. But it was her time to be born, and the pain returned—shooting, crashing, ripping through my back.

I was holding on to my husband's arm, using it to diffuse some of the pain. To be accurate, I was practically breaking his arm, alternately begging him to make the pain go away and apologizing for complaining. I thought that by some miracle he could stop the pain. He was the only one whom I trusted to listen to me. Although Rick didn't experience the pain firsthand, he felt it through my hands and my eyes; there wasn't a contraction that he didn't feel.

When the doctor came back into the room and saw what was happening, he said, "Take it easy. You're going to break that poor guy's arm." By this time, I was clawing at Rick, ripping at his shirt. I just wanted everything to stop. I kept gasping, "I'm going to die, I'm not going to live." At that point the pain was so quick and furious that I had no chance to catch my breath.

"You'll be okay," Rick said reassuringly. His voice was calm, but his arm and his hands were shaking and I could see fear in his eyes. "Try the breathing. I can't do anything for you, Mary," he said softly. "I wish I could."

The doctor raised me to a sitting position. I sat with pillows behind me, my feet in stirrups, and my knees up to my shoulders. I was no longer resisting the birth. When the doctor told me to push, I pushed so hard that I almost passed out. "Bear down," he said, and I bore down with all my heart and strength. Every vein in my neck was popping; every muscle in my body felt as if it were ripping. Suddenly I saw the baby's head. The doctor turned her, and I saw her eyes. As he pulled her out of me, I heard her first cry of life. I reached out my arms and welcomed her to the world.

Sara's birth was different from anything I'd ever gone through before. With my son, Ryan, and my daughter Tuesday, I had not had natural childbirth. With Ryan I had had spinal anesthesia. Tuesday was delivered five minutes after I arrived at the hospital. I hadn't watched their deliveries or had my husband beside me. When you are sixteen or seventeen and having a baby, everyone looks at you as if you are too young. But when you are twenty-nine and your husband's at your side, there is a whole different chemistry. This time I experienced the process with all its pain and beauty and with the maturity to understand how marvelous it was.

"My God, look at the weight of this baby," the doctor said as he held her up. Later he told me that he had expected her to be about seven pounds. It turned out she was nine pounds, two ounces, but she looked even heavier because she was only twenty inches long. He rested her on top of me and cut the cord. She was just beautiful. Perfect in every way, with a full face, blond hair, and beautiful blue eyes. She looked almost exactly the same as my ten-year-old daughter, Tuesday, had looked. I had never expected that.

She lay peacefully in my arms, with her eyes open, looking at me. Her head was perfectly round, her skin soft and purple. "Just look at the color of her," Rick said. His eyes were shining and his voice was full of wonder. He had never seen anything like this before. Watching a birth on TV or in a movie, or hearing about a birth, is not like being there. Seeing Sara born was the turning point in both our lives.

As many times during the nine months as I might have spoken to her as if she were a baby—I mean silly things like bumping my belly against the counter when I was doing dishes, patting it, and saying, "I'm sorry"— she just didn't seem like a baby. Oh, I heard the heartbeat. I saw the sonogram. I felt the fluttering and then the kicking—but it was not like hearing my daughter cry. I just couldn't visualize a baby. I don't think anybody can. She wasn't real to me until I was actually holding her in my arms and hugging her.

I looked at Rick; he was crying. I was crying too. Not because of the pain, but because of the joy. I was so excited, so overwhelmed by the beauty of my daughter and the whole experience of the birth. I cradled her in my arms. Rick was holding me; I was holding the baby. Rick touched her hand, and her tiny fingers curled around his. "I love her, Mary Beth," he said, tears streaming down his face. "I love her because she's a part of you."

The nurse took us to a room. Rick helped me put on a nightgown. There was another woman sharing the room. She had given birth to a baby girl the day before. She had nursed her older child and offered to teach me how to nurse my baby, but Sara didn't need much help. She loved to nurse. She sucked so eagerly that I could hardly believe it.

Already, flowers had begun to arrive. There was a bouquet from my mother and father, a beautiful arrangement sent by the people at Rick's job, and potted pink tulips brought by my sister-in-law. The room was filled with flowers and balloons. It looked like a real celebration. No one at the hospital realized that this was a baby I was having for another couple. Who could imagine that any-one would have gone through this for someone else? But that is what I had agreed to do.

# Chapter 2

# The Infertility Center

She signed a paper, didn't she? Well, so did slave sellers; so did indentured servants who virtually sold themselves into slavery for a term of years; so did long-ago impoverished parents who sold their daughters into brothels. And every day in this country, contracts are entered into for drug deals, murders for hire, arson, insurance scams, illegal gambling, and, yes, child selling. . . . A deal is a deal, right, Your Honor?

—Richard H. Rosichan in *The New York Times*,
April 4, 1987 (letter to the editor)

**T**wo years earlier, on March 30, 1984, I had responded to a newspaper advertisement in the *Asbury Park Press* asking for women willing to help infertile couples bear children.

I had always believed that we were in this world to help other people. I thought that this was something I could do to improve the lives of an infertile couple and at the same time help my own family economically. It seemed like a good way to provide extra opportunities for my children. I reasoned that it would help to pay for their college educations. But most important was the fact that, at that time, I genuinely believed that this was a way for me to help to better the world.

I had once seen a film that had stayed in my mind. It was the story of a woman who had carried an infertile woman's egg and ultimately given birth to a baby. During the pregnancy she had some conflict, but when she saw how much the baby looked like its mother, she knew it was not her baby. She gave it to the real mother and both women were very happy.

When I saw the advertisement, I thought it was the same arrangement. I assumed that the procedure included implanting the woman's egg as well as the man's sperm, and that it actually enabled the infertile couple to have their own genetic child. My sister was unable to become pregnant, and she was suffering terribly. I showed her the ad and I asked her if she wanted me to try to have a baby for her. She declined, saying she was still hoping to become pregnant herself. I had always been religious, and at some level I hoped and I certainly prayed that if I did this for another childless couple, God would reward me by giving my sister a baby. In retrospect, I guess that sounds foolish, but I think that many of us, in the privacy of our own thoughts, have tried to make deals with God.

In any case, I called the number in the advertisement. They sent me an application. It took me about a week to fill out the forms. I mailed them back on a Friday; they called the following Monday and told me I had been accepted. On Tuesday I walked into a posh fourteenth-floor office between Fifth and Madison avenues in New York City. I noticed the expensive furniture, oriental rugs, and prime New York location, and I felt reassured that the business was respectable. As I waited, I leafed through catalogs filled with photographs and brief descriptions of about a hundred available women. From these picture books, childless couples were expected to choose their surrogate mother based primarily on what she looked like.

I was greeted by a warm, friendly, down-to-earth administrator who told me that she herself was infertile and that it took a very special woman to have "another couple's baby." Then I followed the administrator down the hall and naïvely entered the inner offices of Noel Keane, lawyer, former saloon operator, and millionaire baby broker.

Wealth was something new to Keane, the third son of an immigrant father who had come from Ireland to work in Henry Ford's factories. Later I learned that Noel Keane had been indicted for "ambulance chasing" in 1973, when it was alleged that police were funneling accident victims to him. Soon after those charges were dismissed, Keane began his surrogate business in a nondescript brick building on a back street in Dearborn, Michigan. The sign outside said simply LAW OFFICE.

Keane's specialization in surrogate parenting had become a full-time practice. He ran the most lucrative, largest-volume surrogate business in the world because his was the fastest and most accommodating place to rent the womb of a surrogate mother and buy the baby she ultimately bore. For each deal Keane arranged, he personally received $10,000. The mother was paid a fee of $10,000, but only if she gave birth to, and surrendered, a healthy baby. If the baby was deformed, retarded, or damaged in any way, the couple could call the deal off, keep most of the surrogate's $10,000, and return the baby to her. But even when that happened, Keane's $10,000 fee was nonrefundable. Noel Keane publicly claimed he had arranged three hundred births in the year I was pregnant with Sara; at $10,000 each, that figure indicates he received and accepted about $3 million in fees for *his* services.

Infertile couples and others wanting ready-made children traveled from across the country and even overseas as word of Keane's center spread by radio, television, and advertisements in newspapers and magazines. Since its inception in 1976, Keane's business had remained unregulated and uninspected. Unlike other infertility centers, which reject a large number of applicants, Keane accepted 85 to 90 percent. Dr. Philip Parker, Keane's chief psychiatrist, had refused only one of five hundred surrogate mothers. "I have a moral objection to screening out people," Parker said.

In part because of the lack of adequate psychological and medical screening, myriad problems ranging from birth deformities to paternity suits surfaced. I now know that at least ten of Keane's former clients, contacted by a Gannett News Service reporter, expressed bitter dissatisfaction with the program.

Judy Stiver, a surrogate mother from Lansing, Michigan, delivered a retarded baby. She has sued Keane, claiming that he allowed her to be artificially inseminated by a man whose sperm she says contained a herpes-related virus that damaged the baby's brain. Doctors for Keane have conceded in depositions that they do not test the sperm donor because "he is the one that wants the child." The trial court has dismissed Stiver's suit on the ground that Keane was not liable under these conditions, but her lawyer says he will appeal the decision.

Another woman, whose lawsuit was later dismissed on a technicality, filed suit under the name of Jane Doe, blaming Keane for arranging the pregnancy that resulted in the death of her premature baby. She says that despite a medical history of five miscarriages, Keane "coerced" her into joining the program. Keane called this charge ridiculous. He in turn sued her for libel, but later withdrew his suit.

Unaware of the Infertility Center's history and methods, I entered Noel Keane's office on that March day in 1984 with excitement and enthusiasm. The clinic's staff told me how wonderful I was. They said, "This couple will thank you for the rest of their lives and will always think of you. When the baby is older, it will know you brought it into the world and it will have the highest respect for you."

Looking back, I now believe that the praise was a form of brainwashing. Over and over, the staff told me that it was the "couple's baby." They never explained that I would be doing everything that a woman does to produce her own child, including providing half of the genetic inheritance, a fact regarded by the judge as an important argument on behalf of Bill Stern. They never said that it was Betsy who would actually be the surrogate mother, since she was the one who wished to substitute for me. And, in what I felt was their gravest omission, they never told me that Betsy Stern was not infertile, that she had simply chosen not to risk the possibility of aggravating a mild case of self-diagnosed multiple sclerosis. They never said she had not even tried to become pregnant. Nor did they ever call Bill Stern a sperm donor, although in fact each time we went to the Center together, he walked into a small, private room, while I waited outside, and came back a few minutes later carrying his semen in a small jar.

I questioned the doctor during one of the insemination procedures and asked her if she felt that what I was doing was all right. She quickly replied that I was only giving away one egg, and that men regularly parted with millions of sperm. The concept of an egg remained a meaningless abstraction. I didn't think of it as the genetic substance of my child. *No one* ever said to me, "It's your baby, and there's a possibility that when she grows up and finds out you sold her, she might hate your guts." No, they didn't tell me that, and they didn't tell me it was Ryan and Tuesday's baby sister, and they didn't tell me how my husband would feel after taking care of me during the nine months of pregnancy. None of this was mentioned. It was just shoved under the rug. They just kept referring to the "couple's child." It wasn't until the day I delivered my daughter that I fully comprehended the fact that it wasn't Betsy Stern's baby. It was the joy, and the pain, of giving birth that finally made me realize I wasn't giving Betsy Stern *her* baby, I was giving her *my* baby.

I have always been a spontaneous person who wanted very much to please other people—perhaps so much so that it's a flaw in my personality. By the time the clinic completed its screening, I was so anxious to help and so convinced that the child wasn't mine that I didn't even think about the terms of the contract. I even told the Sterns I didn't want the money.

My husband, Rick, on the other hand, hadn't liked the idea very much from the start. At first he thought it would make him look like less of a man. Then he became concerned about how I would react physically to the pregnancy and if I'd be too tired or too ill to take care of the children and cook and clean. Slowly he began to think of it as something generous and nice. Rick had always been behind me, and supportive whenever I wanted to do things for other people. However, he did feel that it would be wrong for us to go through all this and then refuse the money.

I should add that later Rick said in no uncertain terms that there was no way we could sell the baby sister of Tuesday and Ryan. He had simply never thought of it that way. In the times of our worst poverty, if you had asked us to sell one of our children to increase the family budget, we would have thought you were kidding. The idea would have sounded so crazy that we wouldn't have believed it and we certainly wouldn't have considered it. The children were always the most important thing in our lives, but at the time, as I said, we simply didn't think of this baby as mine or ours, we thought of it as "theirs."

When the clinic's psychologist, Joan Einwohner, interviewed me, she must have asked me questions that bordered on reaching past what I was denying. I don't remember much about the interview, but I now know that she was struck by my strong maternal instincts and my love for my two children. And she was worried. Einwohner wrote, "She expects to have strong feelings about giving up the baby. It would be important to explore with her in somewhat more depth whether she will be able to relinquish the child at the end." However, instead of cautioning me, the Center told me that I had "passed" the test. They said that everything was fine.

Later in the pregnancy, when Betsy Stern began calling my doctor and ordering me to stay in bed, I started to pull back from some of the illusions and began to resent the idea that she had rented my body to produce a child. I began to ask questions and express reservations. At that time, I was assured by Sol Radow, the attorney referred to me by the Infertility Center, that if for any reason I ever changed my mind, despite the contract, no court could ever take the baby away. This was the very same position that Keane had publicly expressed three years earlier in *The Surrogate Mother*, his book on surrogate parenting. At that time he wrote, "Any and all contracts between adoptive couples and others wanting children and their surrogate mothers are *unenforceable*. There is," he continued, "no guarantee that the surrogate mother will give up her child." I didn't realize it then, but he had probably taken that position because he suspected that the contract that all of us had signed was not legal in New York, New Jersey, or anywhere else in the United States. It was simply a document that he had prepared on a subject where no clear laws existed.

In addition to me, another of Keane's surrogate mothers changed her mind, after learning in her eighth month that the adoptive mother Noel Keane had chosen for her child was actually a transsexual! She kept her baby.

In yet another Keane deal, Patty Nowakowski, a surrogate mother from Michigan, bore twins, a boy and a girl. Shortly before the twins were born, the father and the adoptive mother told Mrs. Nowakowski that they did not want a male. They took only the baby girl from the hospital, as if they were choosing a puppy from a litter. Mrs. Nowakowski kept her son, and recently obtained custody of her daughter as well.

In spite of all these problems, at least until the New Jersey Supreme Court ruling in September of 1987, Noel Keane's business continued to flourish. He said that the publicity of my case brought him more customers than ever. In fact, he was so busy when my case went to trial that he hired a public-relations firm to coordinate his TV and radio appearances.

Chapter **3**

# The Loss

Probably the most stressful and anxiety-provoking act in human existence is the separation of a woman from her newborn infant. The response to this, which humans share with most of the animal kingdom, is an overwhelming combination of panic, rage, and distress.

Who can dare judge the psychological acts and responses of a woman put to such a test? In the present-day United States, what psychologist can claim to have experience with women subject to that experience?

—A. P. Ruskin, M.D., in *The New York Times*,
April 20, 1987 (letter to the editor)

**O**n the evening of Sara's birth, the Sterns came to my hospital room. They seemed cold and standoffish. They offered no congratulations; they brought no flowers. It seemed as though they just wanted to take my baby, leave, and forget that I existed. Later, the Sterns claimed they were deliberately hiding their excitement because no one at the hospital knew of our arrangement. Now, with a nurse at my side, I went with the Sterns and all my other visitors down to the nursery window to look at Sara. The baby was crying, so I went into the nursery and picked her up. I comforted her and then I held her up to the window.

Tuesday was there. For weeks her classmates had been asking her if the baby had been born yet and what we were going to name it. Tuesday had tried to pretend that nothing was wrong, but as she looked at the baby I could see what she was going through. In one sense it was no different from any other child looking at a new baby sister—except that the love was more intense. At the age of ten, Tuesday was more ready than a child of three or four to accept a baby. Younger children often feel jealous when they are brought to the hospital to see a new baby; they have missed their mothers and want to be the focus of attention themselves. Suddenly, Tuesday's eyes filled with tears. She looked at me as if to say, "Mom, don't do this. Don't give my sister away. Don't sell her. Don't do it."

Everyone was commenting on how much she looked like Tuesday. Everybody was excited and bubbling over. The Sterns were just looking. They didn't smile or laugh or say how beautiful she was. I thought she was gorgeous, but they just stood in the shadows. I felt as though they were vultures waiting to move in for the kill, waiting to claim my treasure. Maybe they were offended because she looked like *my* baby. She wasn't supposed to be mine. But was *was* my child. She had my bracelet on her wrist, and I had her bracelet on mine, and I was the only person who was allowed to go into the nursery and get her.

Actually, except for visiting hours, she was rooming in. I only put her in the nursery when I was taking a shower or something of that sort. She didn't like the nursery; she didn't want to be there. She would cry, so I kept her with me day and night. I held her hour after hour, and it was like holding Tuesday again after ten years.

At that point, I thought, What a mistake I've made. I did not want to make the mistake real. I wanted to pretend that it hadn't happened, that this was just my baby and we would share a normal life together. On one level, I felt guilty because of the obligation I believed I had to the Sterns and I was worried about their feelings, but now I also felt a strong obligation to the baby, as any mother would to her child. I think that young girls who give their babies up for adoption often think that the baby will be better off, but I knew my baby wouldn't be better off. My God, I thought, how is she going to feel when she finds out that she was sold for $10,000? She's going to feel like the slaves did.

On Saturday morning, my roommate was getting ready to go home. Her baby was jaundiced and the doctor didn't know if she could take her home that day. She was crying, and she was upset, as any mother would be. And there I was, thinking, How can I be doing this?

In the next room, a fourteen-year-old unmarried girl had just delivered a little boy and she was keeping him. God, this girl is fourteen, I said to myself. She is keeping her baby. I'm twenty-nine years old and this is *my* baby and these people want to take her away.

Noel Keane had called me a surrogate mother, but now I clearly understood that I was the natural, biological mother. Bill Stern had supplied the sperm, so genetically he was the father, but Rick was my husband and my lover. He was there for the delivery. He watched that baby be born. He was delighted with her, just as he was with Ryan and Tuesday.

I now wonder about the whole concept of what makes someone a father, and how he feels when he sees his child. Do men look at their children and love them because they are a product of their sperm or because they are a part of their wives? Are we to believe that it is just sperm that makes a man a father? And if that is so, then why have we decided that if a married woman is artificially inseminated under usual circumstances, the baby is her husband's child, not the sperm donor's? Is this different because of intent? Because Bill Stern didn't intend to make a donation? Does that change the law and make him a father?

Bill Stern wasn't there when I couldn't get out of bed. He wasn't there when I was throwing up over a toilet bowl on Christmas morning. Rick was. Rick didn't promise to come into the bathroom and put his arms around me when I was throwing up. Rick didn't promise to help me get out of bed or shave my legs or put on my sneakers and tie them. Rick didn't make these promises. Neither did Bill Stern. So either I would have walked around with my sneakers untied and been throwing up in the bathroom by myself or Rick would have been there—and Rick was there. He was the one who was there when I got into bed at night and the baby was kicking and moving and would kick right through my stomach to his back. He was the one who felt that, not Bill Stern.

As I said, I don't know what makes a father, but at that point on that Saturday in April, I knew that I just didn't want to leave the hospital and come home and give my daughter away. I wanted that hospital stay to last forever. My friends were calling and I couldn't pretend anymore. I would just say, "I don't want to talk about it"; "I can't do it"; "I don't know what I'm going to do." So at that point, everybody knew. Slowly but surely, the news was starting to circulate that Mary Beth had made a terrible mistake and was probably going to keep the baby.

When my roommate left on Saturday, I let down my wall. That was when everything came out. I called Rick at work and asked him to come right away. I asked him not to go home first because I needed him now. When I hung up with Rick, the phone rang. It was Betsy Stern. She said that the Infertility Center had messed up, and in order for me to get my $10,000 they had to bring a notary to the hospital. I didn't want the $10,000; I didn't want the notary. I just wanted my baby. I was crying as I said, "Betsy, I don't want the ten thousand dollars. I don't want to talk about this," and I hung up.

The nurse came in. I had the baby lying on my chest, sleeping. I was sobbing. She thought it was the blues, the baby blues. She looked at me and said, "That's okay, cry. It's good to get it out. Don't worry about it."

When Rick came in, I was weeping. Rick sat on the bed with me. "What can I do?" He shook his head and said, "I don't know what we're going to do." Then he put his arms around me. I was looking to him for answers, and he didn't know what they were. I kept crying and repeating, "What can I do? I can't give her away. I can't give her up." And if I said it once, I said it a hundred times.

That night, the Sterns came back. I wanted them to say, "Mary Beth, we can't take your baby away from you," but they didn't say it. They wouldn't say it. I wanted to make them realize that this was my baby and I couldn't give her up. I couldn't give her away or sell her. I told them I didn't think I could go through with it, and Betsy said, "You can visit. You will be like a sister." "I don't want to be the baby's sister," I explained through my tears. "I want to be the baby's mother, which I am. You're asking me to do something that I know isn't right. It's unnatural and I know it's something that I shouldn't be doing."

At that point the Sterns offered me more money. They said, "You keep the money for the delivery." My insurance company was supposed to reimburse me, and I was going to give the money to them. I thought their offer was very generous, but it didn't sway me one bit from wanting to keep my baby. Actually, one side of me thought it was touching, and the other side was almost insulted that they thought they could offer me more money for my child. That wasn't why I was doing the whole thing to begin with.

I looked at Betsy Stern and thought to myself, "Betsy, I'm not selling this child. I started this when I actually believed it *wasn't* my child. Everyone had convinced me that it was your child, but going through the pregnancy and the pain of labor, and then seeing the baby has made me realize that this is *my* baby, not yours, mine." But I didn't say anything. I just burst into tears.

We left the hospital on Easter Sunday morning. My mother had bought the baby an outfit to come home in. Sara wore a pink and white bunting, a white eyelet hat, and an Easter bunny blanket. Everything fit her perfectly and the nurse took her and paraded her around the hospital and everybody was thrilled. She was the center of attention because of the Easter bunnies all over her outfit.

They wheeled me down to the car in a wheelchair. I was holding the baby. Rick had taken all the flowers and gifts down in a cart because there were so many. We got into the car. The sun was shining. It was eleven o'clock, and the Sterns were coming to our home to take her away at two.

On the way home, I spontaneously decided to stop and show Sara to my brothers, who were living together on a farm nearby. I wanted them to be able to see her because I was afraid that none of us would ever see her again. The Sterns were coming in less than three hours, and the deadline was ripping at me all the way home. When I got out of the car, I saw how excited my sister-in-law and two nephews were to see the baby. I had never expected that. I didn't realize that anyone would think of Sara as my baby. But my nephew, who was only three years old, knew it was his cousin. My sister-in-law took her. I was crying. My brother put his arms around me and said, "Oh, Mary, I knew you couldn't do it. What are you going to do?"

When we got home, my neighbor Sue, her husband, my niece, Joei, and my sister-in-law, Sherri, were there. Tuesday and her best friend, Dana, were also there. Everyone wanted to hold the baby. They all thought they were never going to see her again. It was as if I were sentencing her to death or to be banished. Everybody just couldn't hold her enough. We didn't want to put her down. We just didn't want to be without her.

My friend Sue was taking roll after roll of pictures. Tuesday was kissing the baby and playing with her and changing her and I was just numb. I was going to let two strangers take my daughter simply because I couldn't bear to hurt them. I still kept hoping and praying they were going to walk in and say, "We can't do it. We can't take your baby away from you. As much as we want her, as much as she may be a part of Bill, she is also a part of you, and we can't take your child. You deserve to keep her, if that's what you want to do."

But that's not what they did. They came in, they sat on the couch, they didn't know how to hold her, and they couldn't wait to get out of there. They just wanted to take my child. I had refused the money, but they still wanted to take what they had planned to buy and leave. It was as if they were at a car dealership and they were saying, "Just give us the merchandise and we're leaving." I knew it wasn't the right thing, and I knew in my heart I would never get over it. But they were trying to make me feel as though something was wrong with me for wanting to keep my child.

They got up to leave. I went with them to the door. "I always knew the day would come when you would be left empty-handed," Bill admitted sadly. I watched as he put Sara in a baby seat in the back of the car. I looked at her alone in the seat, all curled up like a little rubber ball. Then, as I stood at the door, they drove away.

I collapsed on my front steps. Rick practically carried me into the house. My friend Sue put her arms around me and urged me to come next door to her house for Easter dinner. She thought it would take my mind off the baby. I was trying to pull myself together, and I went over there. But every time I looked at anybody, I burst into tears.

Sue's in-laws were there. They told me I had done a beautiful thing and I would be okay. I just kept crying because I knew it wasn't a beautiful thing for me to give away my baby. I tried to eat, but I couldn't put even a mouthful of food in my mouth. I left and went home. I was upsetting everyone.

Tuesday stayed and spent the night there. I didn't want Tuesday to see me so upset. She knew something was really wrong. She knew a really unnatural thing had taken place. She didn't want to be a part of it.

Rick tried to comfort me. He tried everything he knew. Nothing worked. I didn't want to talk. I didn't want to live. I didn't think Rick felt good about putting his arms around me, even though he was trying to comfort me, because the reason he was trying to comfort me was the wrong reason. You don't comfort somebody who is giving away her child.

Everybody said, "You have two other children." It wasn't as if my baby were dead. My child was alive, and I had given her to two strangers. How could anyone feel that giving away my child was the right thing? I can't imagine that. I just can't.

The Sterns and the Infertility Center had told me I was doing a beautiful thing, but I wasn't. All the way through my pregnancy, I had tried to believe it. I had suppressed the reality; I had denied my feelings. I had not allowed myself to deal with it.

But now I couldn't pretend anymore. I just didn't want to be a party to it, no matter how much it was going to disappoint them. I couldn't bear to be a woman who gave away her child. I didn't want Rick to love me, or Tuesday and Ryan to love me, or even my dogs to love me, because I knew I wasn't worth loving. I wanted to go back to being Mary Beth Whitehead, the person I was before I got involved in this thing. If I gave away my baby, my life wasn't worth anything, and as far as Tuesday and Ryan went, I was no longer worthy of being their mother.

There wasn't anything left, not in my eyes. I knew I was out of control, but I think anyone having her newborn baby taken away from her would be out of control. I wanted to be in control. I wanted to be able to do it. It wasn't that I wouldn't. I *couldn't*.

I began to feel angry and defensive. My body, my soul, my heart, my breathing, my everything had gone into making this baby. What had Bill Stern done? Put some sperm in a cup. What had Betsy done? Bought some clothes, a box of diapers, and a case of formula. That's not having a child.

My sister Joanne had tried to comfort me by telling me about the baby she had lost. Her baby was dead, mine was alive. I couldn't pretend she was dead. She was alive and living with strangers two and a half hours from my house. How could I be at peace, not knowing when she needed me, not knowing when she was crying?

There are a whole lot of things that you don't know when you leave your child. If you are gone for two hours, the first thing you do when you come home is to say, "Was she okay, did she cry?" I wasn't going to be allowed to do that. Everything was meaningless if I couldn't be there for her. It was all gone.

All I did was sob and cry. I just couldn't stop crying. It just kept coming, and the emptiness that I felt was something I never want to feel again.

Eventually I fell asleep. Suddenly I opened my eyes. The room was dark, and I was lying in a pool of milk. The sheets were full of milk. I knew it was time to feed my baby. I knew she was hungry, but I could not hear her crying. The room was quiet as I sat up in the bed, alone in the darkness, with the milk running down my chest and soaking my nightgown. I held out my empty arms and screamed at the top of my lungs, "Oh God, what have I done—I want my baby!"

Chapter **4**

# "I'm Keeping Her"

Indigence bent Mary Beth Whitehead toward compliance, but she was bolted to her feet and liberated by a much greater force.

—Les Payne in *Newsday*, March 1, 1987

**I** sat at the kitchen table until morning watching the clock. At 7:00 A.M. I dialed the Sterns' number. "I have to see Sara. I need to hold her," I stammered. There was a long silence at the other end of the line.

"What time will you be here?" Betsy finally said; her voice sounded dry and tired.

"I'm leaving now," I answered.

As I was walking out of the house, my sister Joanne called. "I don't want you going there alone," she said. "Pick me up. I'm going with you." Even with Joanne at my side, the two-hour drive to Tenafly, where the Sterns lived, seemed almost endless.

When I finally got there, Bill opened the door. "Betsy's in the shower," he said.

"That's okay," I answered. "It's not Betsy I've come to see." I walked past him, up the stairs, and into Sara's room. She looked very tiny and vulnerable and beautiful. I bent down, picked her up, and held her against me. Suddenly, all of the nightmares of the night before vanished. I was whole again. The feeling of not wanting to live completely disappeared. It was as if my baby had been lost or kidnapped, and somehow, miraculously, I had found her. I was Mary Beth again. I knew then that agreeing to part with my daughter was the biggest mistake I had ever made in my life.

Sara was rooting for my breast. I sat down and began to nurse her. My sister, of course, still assumed I was giving up the baby. "I don't think you should do that," she said abruptly. I looked at her as if she had five heads. "I'm concerned about you bonding," she added, her voice softening slightly. "It's too late," I answered. "I've already bonded."

As I held Sara and nursed her, I knew in my heart that no one could separate us. They could send out the Green Berets, the national guard, the army and the navy, but I wouldn't let anyone take that baby out of my arms again. When Bill and Betsy walked into the room, I said, "I'm taking her home." Betsy narrowed her eyes and looked at me as if I were crazy.

"I'm going to call the social worker at the Infertility Center so he can talk you out of it," she announced.

"Betsy," I said calmly, "there is no talking this baby's mother out of anything."

Bill began to moan. "I lost my mother. I lost my father. I know what it feels like to lose."

"But, Bill," I said as kindly as I could, "my baby isn't lost, she's right here in my arms." He continued talking about the death of his parents.

"Bill," I repeated, "your parents have nothing to do with me wanting my baby." It was as if I were speaking in a different language.

"I've lost everything," he wept, "and now you want to take my baby." He lay down spread-eagled across the stairs.

I hated to see Bill suffering. "Give me a week, just a week," I said, trying to calm him. "I need time to think. I can't think without her. I can't live without her." Bill may have hoped that I would return her at the end of the week, but I think we all knew that I would never be able to part with her. Betsy stared at me and my sister.

"Please don't blame my family," I said. "The decision is mine and no one else's." I kissed them and told them that I was deeply sorry for the pain that this had caused all of us.

Betsy picked up the baby's clothes and angrily handed them to me. "I won't be needing these anymore," she said as she put them in my car. I thanked her, but I knew that even if Sara and I left with nothing, it was more important for us to be together than for me to have undershirts and diapers ready. If I lived in the street with my child, it would have been better than parting with her. I didn't need a brand-new crib. I didn't need a brand-new changing table. I didn't need anything fancy or new. I had my baby, and *she* was the best thing going.

I'll never forget the look of joy on Tuesday's face when she saw her sister. All afternoon she proudly brought in one friend after another to show them our new treasure. When

Rick came home from work, he picked up the baby and kissed her. Then he hugged me. "I'm proud of you," he said. Everyone was happy. It seemed to us, in the heyday of our joy, that we would never lose her again, that we were picking up the pieces of our lives and moving forward.

I called my parents in Florida and told them I was keeping the baby. All during the pregnancy I had said that she was not my baby. Now I knew that I had deprived them too. I explained that genetically Sara was *my* daughter and not the product of Betsy's egg, as I had originally thought. "I want to bring her down to see you," I added. I knew that when they saw her they would feel like real grandparents toward her, and I wanted them to feel that way. But most of all I wanted my son, Ryan, who had been staying with them, to see his new sister.

The next day I flew down to Florida with Sara. As soon as we arrived, my mother rushed the baby off to the car. She was so excited and so protective that she was afraid people would breathe on Sara and give her germs.

Ryan, who, at twelve, was often shy and unexpressive, was fascinated. He couldn't get enough of her. "Can I hold her now? Can I hold her now?" he asked constantly. And as I watched my son tenderly holding my daughter, there was a brief and treasured illusion that we were just another ordinary family rejoicing in the birth of our new baby.

Unfortunately, the illusion was short-lived. That night the phone rang. It was Joanne. "The Sterns have been calling constantly," she said. "They've been harassing me and the rest of my family." I telephoned Bill and Betsy and tried to reassure them. I told them that Sara was fine, and that I would be returning home soon.

My mother became alarmed by the conflict. She told me the story of "The Wisdom of Solomon." It was her way of trying to make me see the Sterns' side and comfort me by explaining that Sara would have economic advantages if she lived with them. My mother meant well, but I was hurt and disappointed that she didn't tell me unequivocally not to give my daughter away. Even without her initial support, I knew what I had to do. I also knew I couldn't do it by staying in Florida.

I returned to New Jersey. Rick and Tuesday met me at the airport. As soon as I got back to the house, I called the Infertility Center and spoke to Noel Keane. "I can't give this baby up," I said. "Go for counseling and charge it to the agency," he suggested. "I don't need counseling," I answered. "I *know* what I'm doing. The girls who give away their babies are simply in a deeper state of denial."

Next I telephoned the lawyer whom I had been referred to by the Center. "What are my rights under the law?" I asked. "You are the mother," he told me, "and there is nothing anyone can do about that. The most Bill Stern can get is visitation."

At 6:00 A.M., April 12, Betsy called. "You've had us on an emotional roller coaster all week," she said. "I want you to make up your mind and tell us what you're going to do."

The obligation I felt to them was very strong. I was deeply concerned about their feelings. "Betsy," I said as gently as I could, "I've tried to give this baby to you, but I just can't do it. I cannot sign my rights away."

"Well, she is Bill's baby, too," Betsy snapped angrily.

Then Bill got on the phone. "Mary Beth," he said, "we want to see her. Can't we come and see her?"

I was upset. I felt as I had felt three weeks earlier, at the hospital. They seemed to be hovering over me and waiting to take Sara away. Even so, I said come, but come before Rick gets home from work. I felt he had already gone through enough suffering because of this. "Okay, we'll come now," they said.

As soon as I hung up, I became very concerned about the visit. I called my sister-in-law, Sherri, and asked her to come over. "I don't want to be here alone when they come," I explained, "because I'm afraid they are going to try to take the baby." Months later I learned how justified those fears were. The Sterns already had been in touch with three lawyers and had been advised to get possession of Sara.

The Sterns came in and sat down on the couch. I gave Bill the baby to hold, and then I went into the kitchen with Sherri so that they could have some privacy. I could see their reflections in the glass on my oven door. I watched as they whispered and handed Sara back and forth. Then Betsy called out, "Mary Beth, will you come in here?" Her voice sounded hard. She began to talk about the emotional roller coaster again. "You have to make up your mind," she said. "Your week is up."

I knew, as I had known for days, that there was no easy way to make them understand that they couldn't have my baby. When I had tried to soften it, they had wrongly assumed that my decision wasn't firm. Finally I said it in the most honest and direct way I knew how, with three simple words that couldn't possibly be misinterpreted: "I'm keeping her."

First, the color drained from Betsy's face. Then she became violently angry. It was my first taste of Betsy Stern when she didn't get her way. "I'm calling Noel Keane," she shouted. "I'm going to make you talk to him."

"Noel Keane is your attorney, not mine," I answered as calmly as I could, referring to the fact that Noel Keane always represented the "couple's" interests. "Besides," I added, "I've already called the lawyer from the Center, and he's assured me that nobody can take my baby away."

Betsy sat down on the couch again, looking angrier than before. Her arms were crossed and her face was frozen. "I'm not leaving," she announced. There was something in her manner that made me feel as if I were seeing her for the first time. I had said yes to her over and over, but it wasn't until now, when I said no, that her true colors came out. I was frightened and astonished by the change. "It's going to be a long lawsuit," she said. "It's going to cost you twenty thousand dollars. You don't have that kind of money, Mary Beth, so you might as well just hand the baby over now." My hands began to tremble. "You'll be dragged through the mud," she snapped.

"Betsy, why would you want to do that?" I asked, stunned by what this was becoming. Betsy was physically attacking me, pulling at my arms, ripping at my shirt, shouting, "Give that baby to Bill."

Suddenly I doubled over. I could feel myself breathing just as I had when I was in labor. The baby was only twelve days old and my uterus was still contracting. I felt as if I was going to pass out, and I was afraid that if I did, they would steal Sara. I handed the baby to my sister-in-law and said, "Sherri, don't let her out of your arms."

Bill was sitting on the couch, crying and saying, "Betsy, stop. Betsy, don't do this. Betsy, stop." His voice was a monotone. He was trying to influence her, but he seemed to be paralyzed.

I swayed unsteadily as the room began to blur. "Oh, sit down if you are going to pass out," Betsy said, letting go of me. But as soon as I sat down, she ran over to Sherri and tried to take the baby from her.

Sherri never looked up; she just stared straight ahead and held on. Bill was in the doorway. "Betsy, stop. Betsy, stop," he kept repeating.

I was on the edge of the chair barely able to breathe. "Don't do this. Please don't do this," I kept saying.

Bill looked at me. "It's just not fair," he moaned. "You already have two children."

"Bill," I said, "I love her too, she's mine too. Why can't you see that?" He didn't seem to hear me.

Then, unexpectedly, his manner changed. "Betsy, go to the car," he ordered. Betsy, who was still pulling at Sherri, seemed to respond to Bill's altered tone.

"Let Bill hold that baby and I'll put on my coat," she said. Sherri didn't move. "Let Bill hold that baby and I'll go to the car," she added, as if we were making a deal. I was afraid that Bill was going to grab Sara, run to his car, and take off.

"Please don't do this," I begged. "Just go to the car, please, just leave."

Betsy was becoming more and more adamant. "Give Bill that baby! Give Bill that baby!" she kept shouting.

I was becoming weaker and weaker. I could barely breathe. Sharp pains that felt like contractions were shooting through my body. Oh God, I'd better tell Sherri to call an ambulance, I thought, but instead, I said with as much force as I could, "Sherri, call the police."

Suddenly, Betsy stopped shouting. Her expression changed. She stopped pulling at Sherri and the baby. "All right," she said, "we'll leave."

"Yes, we'll leave," Bill echoed.

There was no more crying and there was no more arguing. They just picked up their coats and left. That was April 12. I didn't hear from them or see them again until May 5.

Chapter **5**

# The Sterns' Secret Legal War

Are the cards stacked against her? You bet. The Sterns, with high-powered legal advice, were able to secure temporary custody. They got the baby from the mother with a court order while the mother didn't even have a lawyer . . . and possession is nine-tenths of the law.

—Judy Mann in the *Washington Post*,
February 20, 1987

**A**fter that, I never let Sara out of my sight. Even if she was only on the other side of a wall, I was uneasy. I kept her with me every single second. Rather than leave her with Rick or a baby-sitter while I was shopping, I called my sister-in-law and asked her to get groceries for me.

When I grew stronger, I began to take Sara with me. First I took her to the grocery store. Then one day I took her to a soccer game that Tuesday was playing in. Everybody on the soccer team knew I had been planning to give her up. They were surprised to see her there. When I told them what a terrible mistake I had made, they said, "Oh, Mary Beth, keep her." These were the parents of children on the soccer team, and they didn't really know me. But they knew Tuesday and they had seen what kind of mother I was to her. They felt that it was right for me to keep my child.

One day I heard a knock on my back door. I peeked out fearfully. To my amazement and delight, I saw about ten of the neighborhood women standing there with baby gifts. They filed in, carrying cakes and vegetable dips and all kinds of presents. It was more than a baby shower; it was their way of saying that Sara was accepted.

Unfortunately, not everyone felt that way. Two of my neighbors did not attend the party. They had ostracized me from the day I returned home with the baby and still wouldn't speak to me. Months later, one of the families apologized. I was hurt by their rejection, but touched by the kindness of so many others.

One woman called and said she had a crib and a carriage. Another went up to her attic and collected all of her daughter's baby clothes. I didn't have much money, but Sara always looked like a million dollars. She was a thriving, beautiful baby, and for a wonderful three-week period our house was filled with the joy of new life.

On April 27, when Sara was exactly four weeks old, my dog, Jenny, went into labor. Rick wasn't home from work yet, so I called Sherri again and asked her if she would come over and help me. She had never delivered puppies before, and was stunned by the process. "Oh, Mary, there's so much blood," she kept saying. I was directing her from the top of the stairs while nursing Sara. Together we delivered the first two puppies. By the time Rick came home, Tuesday and about half a dozen of the neighborhood kids were glued to the basement steps watching the process and cheering Jenny on. Nine puppies were born in all.

Shetland sheepdogs are a delicate breed, and require a lot of care. With so large a litter, there was no way that Jenny could provide enough milk. Without our help, I knew that several of the puppies would die. When they were a bit stronger I would be able to feed them cereal and buttermilk in cupcake tins, but for now they would have to be bottle-fed. For a moment, as I held Sara in my arms, I wondered how I would manage. As it turned out, Tuesday and Rick both pitched in and helped, and in spite of all of the work, my life had never been richer.

Throughout this period, I hadn't heard a word from the Sterns. But I knew they would be back. My worst nightmare was of them crawling through a window some night and stealing Sara while I was asleep. I never even imagined the sophisticated, methodical legal war that they were already secretly waging.

Even before Sara was born, a petition by the Sterns to declare Bill Stern her father was filed in a Florida court. They claimed that the artificial insemination was done without Rick's consent. They did this because, under existing law, if my husband had consented to the insemination, Bill Stern would have been declared a sperm donor. Rick would be considered the legal father and Bill would have no claim to Sara. On May 2, 1986, the petition was approved in Florida and a paternity order was entered declaring Bill Sara's father.

The Florida court was used at Noel Keane's suggestion because the procedures there were very loose, even though the Sterns and Rick and I lived in New Jersey. By coincidence, I had just been in Florida and would be there again very shortly, but this had nothing to do with Keane's choice of that state. An answer to Bill Stern's petition, supposedly signed by Rick and me, acknowledging that Bill was the father, had also been filed in the Florida court. But Rick and I had never seen that document. Apparently, a blank page that had been attached to another document that Rick and I had signed at the request of the Infertility Center had then been attached to the answer, unlawfully notarized, and filed in the Florida court. Added to this was the fact that the Florida judge who signed the order had no authority to do so; he happened to be a judge who had no power to handle that kind of case.

In September, our lawyers had the paternity order vacated by a Florida court on the ground that the judge was unqualified to sign the document. But, back in May, the Sterns had used this invalid order to support their request for immediate custody of Sara. This request was submitted to New Jersey Superior Court Judge Harvey Sorkow on May 5, together with several certifications designed to disqualify me as an adequate parent. The certifications said I was suicidal, but didn't explain that I was afraid of losing my child and was reacting to that fear. They also alleged that Rick and I were both unfit parents.

"Defendants Mary Beth Whitehead and Richard Whitehead are unfit to be entrusted with the care, custody, education, and maintenance of said child," one of the documents said. "The happiness and welfare of said child requires that the Plaintiff William Stern be given the child's care, custody, education, and maintenance by judgment of this court." The certification also demanded that the courts strip me of my rights because I had less money and education than the Sterns. It said, "Plaintiff

Elizabeth Stern is occupied as a pediatrician. Plaintiff William Stern is occupied as a biochemist. Plaintiffs are capable of supporting the child to be adopted." At the end of the certifications, the Sterns demanded a judgment terminating my parental rights.

Based on the invalid paternity order and the Sterns' unsupported allegations, an unprecedented *ex parte* order (an order signed without notice to Rick and me) had been issued by Judge Sorkow on May 5. It immediately transferred Sara's custody to Bill Stern and allowed the local police to assist in seizing my baby without warning. Such orders are extremely rare, and are usually reserved for chronic abuse cases after many attempts to work with the family have failed. Even then, the family is normally given the opportunity to be heard by the judge *immediately*.

In our case, the order didn't even allow us to appear before the judge to present our side for twenty-two days. It also mandated that everything be kept under seal. I had absolutely no warning of what was about to happen.

## Chapter 6

# May Fifth

Richard Whitehead has a history of alcoholism. . . . He also
has a history of loyalty in this situation that is borderline
heroic. How many husbands would be willing to put their
families through this kind of purgatory for the sake of
keeping a baby?

—Judy Mann in the *Washington Post*,
February 20, 1987

It was late in the after-
noon on May 5, 1986. I had pork chops and bags of
groceries on the kitchen counter. Rick had just come home
and was in the kitchen with two of his friends. I was
sitting on the living room couch, nursing the baby. Tuesday was sitting beside me. All of a sudden, Tuesday said,
"Mom, it's the police and Betsy and Bill." An image of
our confrontation on April 12 flashed before me.

I panicked, jumped up, and ran out the back door
with Sara in my arms and Tuesday beside me. A policeman grabbed me. "Let her go, let her go," Tuesday
begged. Rick ran out and shouted, "Get your hands off
my wife!" Then Betsy and Bill came running into the yard,

followed by three or four more policemen. I kept looking at Bill and saying, "Please don't do this, don't do this."

Betsy walked up to me. Her face was cold and hard. She held out her arms. "Give me that baby," she demanded.

I couldn't understand why they were doing this, and I kept saying, "Please don't do this," over and over.

When I realized that begging wasn't going to get me anywhere, something in me hardened. "You are not taking my baby. You can't have her," I said. The police were holding me. Betsy was pulling at the baby and Tuesday was screaming, "Get your hands off my mother! Leave my mother alone." Rick was still shouting, "Get away from my wife!" But now his friends were holding him back because the police were threatening to put him in jail.

By this time there were four police cars on my lawn. Strangers were standing on the curb; they probably thought someone had been murdered. My brother and sister-in-law and neighbors had come running over because of the screaming. Tuesday was crying hysterically. She ran over to the Sterns, who had returned to their car, and said, "Please don't take my mom's baby, don't do this, please, take me instead." They wouldn't even look at her. They closed their eyes and shook their heads.

I never thought in a million years that they would treat a ten-year-old child that way. Tuesday was completely beside herself. I had never seen her that way. Not when she walked into a sliding glass door and had to be rushed to a hospital. Not when she fell off a swing and broke her arm. Not when she had salmonella poisoning. I was frightened—not only for Sara and myself, but also by the way Tuesday was reacting.

Betsy began to instruct the police. Everyone came into

the house. The police handed us an order to surrender "Melissa Stern." Rick went into the bedroom, got the baby's birth certificate, and handed it to the police. It identified our baby as Sara Whitehead. I was listed as the mother, and Rick was listed as the father. At that point it was obvious that the police didn't know what to do. No one knew what to do.

I went into the bedroom and huddled there with the baby and the nine puppies. The puppies had been sleeping there because it was not warm enough in the basement. I just kept nursing the baby. I didn't want her to cry and I didn't want her to be frightened by the turmoil that was going on in the house. I was shaking all over— my knees, my legs, my hands. I just couldn't believe that the police were going to take my baby. To this day, I still can't believe that that's the way they did things.

A little while later, Rick heard the police say that they were going to knock me down and forcibly take the baby. He came into the room and held my hand. "Mary," he said softly, "all through the pregnancy we told each other she was not our baby and that we were doing the right thing by giving her up. But now we know we were wrong, and when it comes right down to it, neither of us can let her go." He paused for a minute and then said, "Are you willing to throw it all to the wind and run?" I looked at Sara and then at Rick, and nodded. He kissed me, then walked over to the window and kicked out the bedroom screen.

Without wasting another minute, he walked around to the back of the house. The Sterns and the police were in the front. "Mary Beth, hand her to me," he said as he came to the window. I was so scared that for a moment I was even afraid to give her to Rick. But they were closing in. I could hear the police and Bill and Betsy outside. I felt I had no choice. I pulled Sara away from my breast, wrapped her in a blanket, and handed her to Rick.

With tears streaming down my face, I watched Rick walk away with Sara. He didn't run. He just walked. I stood there until I couldn't see them anymore and I knew they were safely away from the house.

I walked into the living room and held out my hands for handcuffs. "The baby's gone," I said. "If you want to lock me up, go ahead."

"What do you mean, the baby's gone?" the sergeant asked angrily.

"She's gone," I repeated. I think they thought I had killed her. They ran into the house and began searching.

"Nothing better happen to that baby, or your life's on the line," the sergeant yelled. Suddenly a voice blared over the police radio: "Man seen running with infant."

Terrified that Rick and Sara would be shot, I rushed outside and over to the Sterns' car, and held on to the window, which was open about six inches. "Bill, please stop this," I begged.

Betsy was sitting in the backseat. Bill was in front. She took the side of his face and whipped it around toward her. "Don't look at her, Bill. Don't look at her," she ordered.

"Look at me," I pleaded, as I stood there barefoot, in a pink and white nightshirt, with blood all over my legs. I was bleeding more heavily than I normally did, because I was so upset, and in all the confusion I had soaked right through the sanitary napkin.

As I spoke, a police officer grabbed me. He threw me onto the hood of the police car and handcuffed my hands behind my back. The Sterns watched without expression.

Tuesday was desperately screaming, "Bill, help her, please help her," as loudly as she could. The Sterns rolled up the windows of their car and pulled away. The policeman pushed me into the police car and slammed the doors.

I sat in the hot, dirty car with about half an inch of sand under my feet. I still hadn't healed from the baby's delivery and I felt like an open wound. The handcuffs were cutting into my wrists, and I felt as if I were trapped in a coffin and suffocating. Through the window, I spotted my brother Jeffrey, who lived down the block and had run over. I kept calling to him, but he couldn't hear me. "Jeffrey," I cried as loudly as I could, "get me a lawyer!"

Then, unexpectedly, the policemen, who apparently knew they had no legal grounds for holding me, opened the doors of the car. Without an explanation or an apology, they pulled me out, removed the handcuffs, and said roughly, "You're free to go." I staggered back into the house, numb with grief and fear, and waited for Rick to call.

About an hour later, the phone rang. "I'm on my way to my sister Nancy's house," Rick whispered. "Sara's fine. She has my handprint on her back from all the bouncing. But you know what, Mary? She never cried a peep. It's almost as if she knew. Come as soon as you can. She's hungry and she needs you."

The police were still circling the block and knocking on neighbors' doors, searching for the baby. Several of my neighbors called and offered to help me. Together we devised a plan. I put on one of Rick's big flannel shirts and hid my hair in a baseball cap. I threw some clothes into a plastic trash bag, then called my brother and asked him to come down and get the puppies. After it grew dark, my neighbor walked with me to his work van.

Disguised by the clothing, I passed for a workman about to begin a night shift. Once I was safely at my sister-in-law's, my best friend, Barbara, brought Tuesday in her car.

Several days later, when neighbors went in my house, they found the pork chops still on the counter and all the groceries that I had never unpacked still in the kitchen. They said it looked as if an entire family had died.

Sara was asleep when I arrived at my sister-in-law's. I picked her up and held her close to me. I rocked her and kissed her. All I wanted then was to get as far away from this nightmare as I could. I decided that we would all go to my parents' house in Florida and try from there to hire a lawyer and determine what our legal rights were.

I was afraid to fly out of Newark Airport because I thought the police might be watching it. I waited until morning, then had an airport limousine pick us up and take us to the Philadelphia airport. From there we flew directly to Florida and I began my life as a fugitive, trying to keep my baby daughter and running in terror from the law.

Chapter 7

# Life on the Run

While soaring toward new legal horizons, the case reaches
way, way back to test the basic, emotional stuff of
motherhood.

—Les Payne in *Newsday*,
March 1, 1987

**A**s soon as we arrived in
Florida, I began calling lawyers. They all wanted $5,000
retainers. It might as well have been $500,000. We simply
didn't have it. I offered them the only things I could think
of: whatever equity we had in the house and the car. But
each of the lawyers told me that if I couldn't get cash, I
couldn't get their help. I started calling congressmen.
Those I could reach were confused by the situation I
described. They said that the entire surrogate concept was
so new that no laws existed to govern it. They were sorry,
but they couldn't help me.

While I struggled to find legal or political help, I
continued to be deeply concerned about Tuesday. She was

so shaken by what the police had done that she was afraid to let me out of her sight. If I went to the bathroom, she stood outside the door, waiting to make sure that no one attacked me. My own state of mind was not much better. When Rick and my father flew back to New Jersey to get our car, I was so frightened that the police were going to catch Rick and throw him into jail that I was practically a basket case until he returned.

One rainy day when I was just starting to calm down, Rick and I took the kids to a local mall. When we got back, my father was waiting outside. As soon as I saw the expression on his face, I knew that something was wrong. He motioned to us to pull the car into the garage and shut the door. "The neighbors just called," he whispered as soon as we were safely inside. "They said that private investigators are searching for you." I became terrified and decided that we had to leave.

Tuesday and Ryan had just begun to attend school in Florida, and I thought that the stability of my parents' house would be better for them than being on the run with Rick, Sara, and me. Tuesday cried and begged me not to leave. My mother finally told her that I might be put in jail if she didn't let me go. I kissed her good-bye and pulled myself away from her.

We drove to Rick's brother's house with Sara, who was now two months old. As it turned out, we stayed there for only one day. I was afraid that, since his name was also Whitehead, we'd be too easy to track down.

We had no money for a motel—at that point we didn't even have money for food—so we reluctantly imposed on another relative, a cousin and his wife. They were wonderful to us. They gave us our own room and they fed us.

Before this happened, we had been in relatively good financial shape. Things were much easier than they had ever been. We had a house, a new car, and nice furniture. But, naturally, without Rick's weekly income we quickly ran out of money. We could no longer make payments on the car or the house.

I was still calling lawyers every day and being turned down by each one, when I learned that the Sterns had gone back to court on May 27. This time they had obtained an order placing a freeze on whatever was left in our bank account. They had also put a writ of attachment on our house, so we couldn't sell it to raise money for a lawyer. Worst of all, the judge had issued a warrant for my arrest, for the crime of interference with custody.

One evening shortly after May 27, my mother called and said detectives had been following her and Tuesday and Ryan. In desperation, convinced that they were on our trail, we borrowed some money from Rick's brother and my parents and took off again. At first we wandered around the state, panicked and on the run, stopping at motels when we were too exhausted to go any farther.

After a few weeks and about fifteen motels, our money ran out. Fortunately, we had a big family living in Florida and we had always been close. We moved in with my cousin Kevin and his wife, Jules. They had two young children. Jules was a teacher and worked full-time. When she came home I had a meal on the table, her laundry was done, and her house was clean. That's how I repaid her.

Jules told us to stay as long as we liked. She was wonderful and hospitable, but it was a terribly difficult time for me. I was living without a quarter in my pocket. I had two kids more than five hours away. I knew that they missed me and needed me, yet I was afraid to go back to my parents' house. I was always scared to death. At night I lay next to Sara, afraid to sleep. Every time a strange car drove down the street, I began to tremble.

Meanwhile, I knew that my father and mother were having a difficult time dealing with the situation and managing the two kids. I desperately wanted us all to be together again. Finally, I decided that, whatever the consequences, I *had* to return. I hoped that if I went back to my parents' home and kept the car in the garage and stayed in the house, no one would know we had returned.

At first, it seemed to work. Things were calm. No one appeared to be trailing us. Gradually, both Rick and I began to relax. Rick got a job on a garbage truck and another working nights, cleaning a movie theater. The money was horrible, but at least we could make the car payments and we were surviving. Ryan's birthday came and went.

I had Sara christened on June 29, when she was three months old. My aunts came to the christening. They brought presents and tried to be cordial, but I knew they weren't accepting of what I was doing. The priest who christened Sara said that in his eyes the baby was Rick's baby since she was conceived during our marriage to each other. He also told me that he didn't think she could be legally taken from me. After all, he reasoned, I was her mother.

On July 18, at about 9:30 A.M., right after I had given Sara a bath, Tuesday saw a man peering into the sliding glass windows at the back of the house. The baby's walker was in open view, so he obviously knew there was a baby in the house. As soon as he got a glimpse of the walker, he knocked on the window. He pretended he was a neighbor who had lost his dog. "Have you seen a fluffy white dog?" he asked casually.

"No," Tuesday answered.

"Is your mother here? Maybe she has seen my dog," the man pressed.

"Mom," Tuesday called innocently.

I walked into the room, and the minute I saw him I knew we had been caught. I was certain that he was a detective sent by the Sterns. First of all, everyone in my parents' neighborhood was older than he was. Besides, they all walked their dogs on leashes. Trying not to appear shaken, I told him that I hadn't seen his dog. Then I watched as he crossed the street and got into a white Buick. Now I was more frightened than ever.

In desperation, I telephoned Bill Stern and begged him once again not to take Sara from me. "Bill," I said, "she's been breast-fed for four months. Do you want her ripped out of my arms? Do you know how it would traumatize her?"

"Uh-huh," he answered indifferently.

"Bill," I persisted, "we have lost everything. . . . Rick had nothing to do with this, and he has lost everything that he has worked for. . . . Do I have to come back and be thrown into jail?"

"I don't want to see you in jail, Mary Beth," Bill said, ". . . but you have to come back with the baby."

"Bill," I answered, growing more and more agitated, "it seems like you've got all the cards. You've got the money, everything of mine is frozen. Bill, she's my flesh and blood, just as she's yours. She's mine too, and I would have given her up, but I couldn't do it. Why can't you understand that?"

There was silence at the other end of the line. We

continued talking for a few more minutes without getting anywhere. Finally, Bill said, "Our only alternative is to fight for her in court."

"But you've made it impossible for me to do that," I replied. "You know I can't get a lawyer. I'm going to be thrown into jail. I'll tell you what you're doing," I continued, only now I was crying as I spoke. "You are absolutely trapping me. You are leaving me no alternative." I thought of Rick and Ryan and Tuesday. "I've ruined so many people's lives," I sobbed.

Then an image of handing Sara to the police and watching them carry her away flashed before me.

"Things have changed," he said, interrupting my thoughts.

"What has changed?" I asked.

"I'll tell you what has changed," he said. "It's cost us a lot of money."

I felt the anger rise in me. He *has* the money and he will stop at nothing, I thought. He will destroy my husband and children and tear my daughter away from me. "Forget it," I said, out of control now. "I'd rather see me and her dead before you get her. I gave her life and I can take her life away." Of course, I didn't mean it. It was an expression of my desperation, not a threat. And Bill didn't take me seriously—I'm certain of that, because when I called him back the next day he didn't even bother to ask if Sara was okay.

I asked if he had spoken to his lawyer about unfreezing our assets. "Yes," he answered coldly. "The only way you can do this is to have *your* lawyer petition the court. My lawyer won't do it. . . . It's out of our hands."

"That's not true, Bill," I said. "You could dismiss the charges."

"No," he repeated, "you have to have a lawyer petition the court to overturn it."

"Well, how am I supposed to get a lawyer, Bill? All my assets are frozen. A lawyer is not going to take my case without funds."

I was completely trapped in a circular, no-win situation. Bill Stern had me where he wanted me, and he knew it. If there was any strength left in me, it was a streak of defiance. I wanted to let Bill know that I wasn't the only one who could be dragged through the mud. I struck out blindly and came up with the most horrible thing I could think of. I accused him of sexually molesting Tuesday and threatened to report it to the judge if he took me to court. It was another idle threat, made in a moment of desperation. Bill and I both knew that. But only Bill knew that he had secretly tape-recorded our telephone conversations and that months later the comments would be played back in a courtroom and over national television.

I spent the next few days trying once again to retain a lawyer. I finally reached a man who said he would accept a $5,000 third mortgage on my house as a retainer and represent me. I was so relieved that I wouldn't have cared if he was the worst lawyer in the world. At least I had a chance. I could finally stop living as a fugitive. I could return home and *try* to fight back.

The next day, Rick and I loaded the car, gathered the children, and headed for New Jersey. We decided to spend the night with an old friend who lived several hours away, on the west coast of Florida. It would give us a place to sleep and a chance to say good-bye. At that point I still didn't know if I would be thrown into jail.

We arrived about five o'clock in the evening. We had

dinner together and took the kids swimming. As the evening wore on, I developed a backache that seemed to get more and more severe with every hour that passed. I kept Rick awake all night. Nothing I did seemed to relieve it. I went downstairs and took Tylenol. Then I took a bath. I tried sitting, standing, and lying down, but I just couldn't get comfortable.

By morning the pain was excruciating. I also felt sick to my stomach and I had developed the worst chills I had ever experienced. I was shaking so hard from the chills that my teeth were chattering and my knees were knocking together. Rick wrapped blankets around me and I hobbled outside to lie in the sun. For a while the chills and backache subsided, but I still felt very weak. I lay on the couch with the baby beside me and nursed her for what turned out to be the very last time.

Toward afternoon the chills returned with such fury that I asked Rick to call an ambulance. "Mary," he said, stroking my hair tenderly, "you just have the flu."

"No, this is more than the flu," I answered, shivering.

Rick held my hands in his and tried to press some warmth into them. "What do you think is wrong?" he asked.

"I don't know," I managed to say. "I'm so sick—everything hurts so much that I can't even touch my arms."

"You'll be okay," he said softly.

But by the time my friend came home, I was so sick, I don't remember her coming in. I don't remember much of anything after that point. Rick says I sat up on the couch, picked up a glass of Pepsi, took a sip, and then began to throw up in the glass. While Rick was cleaning it up I vomited again all over the couch. "Mary, go to the bathroom!" Rick yelled. "You're throwing up all over the furniture." Obediently, I staggered into the bathroom, still throwing up, and that was it. They say I came crawling out of the bathroom and just lay on the floor. I couldn't hold my head up. I couldn't do a thing. Rick took my temperature and found it to be 105. Alarmed, they decided that they had better get me to an emergency room.

My only memory of being driven to Martin Memorial Hospital in Stewart, Florida, was that it felt like there were razor blades underneath my fingertips. My vision had begun to fail, my knees and feet and hands had become a waxy blur. When I raised my eyes and tried to focus, it looked as though the dashboard on the car had melted.

Finally, after what felt like an almost endless drive, we got to the hospital. Rick lifted me into a wheelchair and wheeled me into the emergency room. The nurse on duty took one look at me and knew something was seriously wrong. She immediately moved me past a waiting room filled with people and put me on the examining table.

By this time I had lost my sight. I kept drifting in and out of consciousness. I remember someone bringing Rick into the room and saying, "Do you know this man?" Rick touched my hand but I couldn't see him. I was totally blind. My speech was gone. I could hear someone saying, "Who is the President of the United States?" but I couldn't respond. Then I heard a man's voice say, "Mr. Whitehead, we are going to have to do a spinal tap."

"Oh no, don't do that," Rick answered.

"If we don't do a spinal tap, your wife will die," the voice insisted.

"Then do it," Rick said.

As it turned out, a severe kidney infection had made

poisonous substances back up into my bloodstream, causing sepsis and very high fever. The condition was called toxic encephalopathy with pyelonephritis.

I woke up in a CAT scan machine with a nurse standing nearby. "You're okay. Just lie there, we're almost done," the nurse said. I looked up at her and then I passed out again. The next time I woke up, I was in Intensive Care. A priest had come in to give me last rites. Another nurse was standing beside the priest. Both of them were talking to me, but I couldn't absorb what they were saying.

That was July 30. I didn't know it yet, but nearly three months of hiding Sara were about to end. While I was lying in the intensive care unit that afternoon, drifting in and out of consciousness, the Sterns were boarding a flight to Florida. They were armed with a new weapon: another court order, this one authorizing Florida police to search for and forcibly seize my baby.

Rick, who was also unaware of the most recent order, came to the hospital to visit me. I was feeling a little more alert, and I can remember his telling me that he had decided to take all three children back to my mother's house until I was well enough to travel. It seemed like a sensible plan, so I nodded in agreement. Rick left as soon as visiting hours were over. It was a five-hour drive. He arrived at my mother's with the three kids at about 2:00 A.M.

At nine the next morning he was sitting in the kitchen, drinking a cup of coffee before driving back to the hospital. Tuesday was in the bedroom, brushing her hair. My father had just gone out for a bike ride, and my mother was in the garage preparing to do laundry. The garage door was open a foot or two. In Florida, people leave their garage doors partially open so that the air can circulate.

Three uniformed police crept through the opening in the garage door. Without explanation, they grabbed my mother, knocked her down, and held her helpless on the ground. Rick looked up sleepily as an older man in plain clothes, with a stocky build and graying hair, walked through the front door and toward the bedroom. He assumed it was one of my parents' friends.

Suddenly, Tuesday's piercing scream echoed throughout the house. "Don't take her, that's my sister, put her down!" A moment later, Rick saw Tuesday running frantically after the man, beating him with her hairbrush. Rick rushed into the living room, but as he approached, the man lifted the baby over his head and held her, what seemed to Rick, dangerously close to a rotating ceiling fan. Sara began to scream. Fearful that she would be caught in the whirling blades of the fan, Rick hesitated. "I've got her!" the man shouted as two or three uniformed police and two plainclothesmen ran into the house.

In a matter of seconds the man holding Sara had passed her to the uniformed police. They in turn had passed her to a woman who sat in a car waiting nearby. They threw a piece of paper containing their orders onto the grass and jumped into their cars. Tuesday stood on the front lawn, crying, "You can't do this, you can't take her," as Rick began to chase the police cars down the street. But he knew it was hopeless. Alone and empty-handed, he turned back and walked toward the house.

My mother was stunned and furious. She kept saying that she couldn't believe that this had happened in the United States of America. She couldn't call the police because they were part of it. Not knowing what else to do, she picked up the telephone and called the local newspaper.

Rick was heading back to the hospital, agonizing over how to break the news to me, when my sister Sharon called. The first thing I said was, "How's the baby?"

"Oh, Mary," she stammered, "I don't know how to tell you this." Then she began to cry.

I still wasn't thinking clearly, but, weak as I was, the second I heard my sister's cry, I knew. I just *knew* they had gotten her. "Those sons of bitches," I moaned.

That evening an article appeared in the *St. Petersburg Times*. By the next day, word of the situation had spread like wildfire. Reporters were calling from all over the country. TV crews began to arrive at the hospital. NBC came first, then ABC and CBS. The doctor said I was too ill to be interviewed. He was afraid I would have a relapse. I was still on an IV. My face and body were bloated from the poisons that had backed up into my bloodstream. I didn't have any makeup on, and I still had vomit in my hair, but I let the reporters and TV crews come in. *Finally*, someone was willing to listen.

Soon afterward I received a letter from the lawyer who had agreed to represent me. He had changed his terms. Now he said that in addition to the $5,000 third mortgage I had agreed to, he wanted 25 percent of all book, film, and magazine article rights to my life. I was shocked and disturbed by his attitude. All I wanted was my baby. Within a few days, half a dozen other lawyers had contacted me. Now they were coming out of the woodwork and offering their services. I called one of them back. Alan Grosman flew down to Florida to meet with me, and warned me that if I didn't keep the story in the media, I'd lose my baby. He seemed kind and intelligent, and I signed an agreement with him that afternoon.

As soon as I was discharged, we headed over to my mother's house to pick up Tuesday and Ryan. But, by the time we were halfway there, I felt almost as sick as the day I entered the hospital. I rode with my head in Rick's lap.

When we finally arrived, a television crew and the press were in the driveway. "Oh no," I said to Rick, "I'm too sick." Rick half carried me into the house. I lay down on the couch. My fever had risen again. I was throwing up, and I could feel myself drifting away. Finally I said, "Call an ambulance." My mother panicked. She was so upset that I thought she was going to have a heart attack. I kept saying, "Calm down, Mother, calm down, just get an ambulance." When the ambulance arrived, Channel 13 filmed me being lifted into it. Once I was inside, paramedics immediately hooked up an IV. They flushed my system, which had become dehydrated from all the vomiting, and once again rushed me to the hospital.

Slowly, very slowly, I began to recuperate. But for days, strings of mucus kept running out of me. It wasn't diarrhea—it was all the contaminating bile that had built up in my system. It was like nothing I had ever experienced before.

Between bouts of acute illness, I kept pumping the milk from my breasts so that when I recovered and got Sara back, I could still nurse her. I missed her terribly, and her safe return was the dream that kept me going. I was still too weak to travel, but I was determined to recover as quickly as possible. All I could focus on was the desperate desire to get home so that I could continue in earnest what had now become my public fight for Sara.

# Chapter 8

# Looking Back

Motherhood . . . has a history and an ideology . . . yet nothing had prepared me for the intensity of the relationship already existing between me and the creature I had carried in my body . . . held in my arms and fed from my breast.

—Adrienne Rich in *Of Woman Born*

**N**othing in my background had prepared me for the battle I was about to wage. All my life I had wanted to be a mother. I had grown up believing that the purpose of my life was to have children. As the sixth of eight children, with three older sisters, I had learned early that a girl's place in the family was very different from a boy's.

My father was a hard-driving and intelligent man, a junior high school math and science teacher who often spent summers and vacations going to graduate school, while my mother stayed at home with the children. He was a powerful man with an occasional impatient streak. Sometimes, if he'd had a bad day at school, he'd come home and take it out on us. If one of us did something wrong, he'd be angry at the whole family. Still, he was clearly our leader. The rest of us looked up to him and admired his broad range of interests. As much as he valued learning, he never neglected the other aspects of his life. To this day he has remained a thin, handsome, and athletic man. He still plays softball with the boys.

My mother, an attractive, brown-eyed redhead, was as energetic as she was feminine. In addition to being the mother of eight, she was a hairdresser and beautician. When we were very young, she would not go to work until late in the afternoon, when my father got home from school. As we grew older she began to work full-time, leaving my sister Joanne to take care of us.

Joanne not only took care of us but also did much of the housekeeping. When I was about six and too young to help with the housework, I would often sit outside the house while she did the cleaning so as not to get in the way.

One day, Mike, an old man who lived across the street, saw me sitting there. He invited me into his house. That day was the beginning of a friendship that lasted until his death. Mike had no children of his own, and over the years he and his wife became like grandparents to me. I frequently ate meals at their house and spent the night there. They even fixed up the bedroom on the top floor for me. I used to stay there as often as my parents would allow.

I had always been unhappy that my mother worked and could not be at home with me. As I grew older, that unhappiness, combined with the memory of my sister's harshness, made me vow that I'd be a different kind of mother. I'd wash and clean and iron just as my sisters had, but I'd be warm and kind like my mother, and, most important of all, I'd be available. I'd always be there at home for my children whenever they needed me. I wanted to be the ideal mother with the storybook house and the picture-perfect children.

As soon as my sisters grew up and left home to go to college or get married, I began to play the role of the substitute mother to my younger brothers. I would cook the dinners, do the scrubbing, cleaning, and ironing, lay out my brothers' school clothes, and make their lunches. At age eleven, I loved playing the mother so much that I thought it was the only thing I would ever want to do. If I had had my way, I would have stopped going to school immediately and been a little housewife forever.

I was entirely comfortable in that role and very uncomfortable in school. I hated the cliquishness of the girls in my classes and the way the teachers seemed to favor some of the children and ignore others. I felt out of place and ill at ease.

Part of my problem dated back to an accident that had occurred when I was in second grade. We were all stuck at home with chickenpox. My little brother Rick, who was four at the time, was playing with a toy gun. I was standing behind him, when suddenly he drew the gun from the holster and accidentally hit and broke two of my permanent upper teeth. The pain was intense. I'll never forget running across the street to Mike's house and seeing the trail of blood in the snow. I was taken to a doctor and then to a dentist, but at that time, they didn't have the cosmetic dentistry that they have now. The dentist just looked at my front teeth broken in an ugly V, and sent me home. From second grade to eighth grade, the kids at school made fun of me and called me a vampire. For a while the dentist put a silver cap on one of the teeth because the nerves were exposed. That looked even worse. It also fell off whenever I ate crunchy food. After a while I vowed never to smile or to eat in school. Home was the refuge from the discomfort of feeling like a misfit in school.

I believed that being a mother and taking care of children was my calling in life. I eagerly awaited the day I could do it full-time. When I was fifteen I told my parents I didn't want to go to school anymore. The idea was especially difficult for my father to accept. But both of my parents knew how unhappy I had always been in school, and although they didn't approve of it, they finally agreed that it was probably best for me. They reluctantly signed the consent forms.

I immediately went to work in my brother Donny's luncheonette. Five years earlier, Donny had been wounded in Vietnam. He had been hit with a grenade and was badly injured. After surgery, he eventually recovered, but it took a long time.

Donny was a good-looking guy with dark hair, blue eyes, and an easy manner. We had always gotten along well together. The fact that he was still weakened from his injury and needed my support just drew us closer. I enjoyed helping him. I made sandwiches, waited on customers, cleaned tables, and had coffee ready when we opened at five every morning to serve breakfast to the truck drivers.

When I first met him, Rick Whitehead drove an asphalt truck. He often came in with his buddies. He was a shy, lonely man who would sometimes linger and talk to me. I sensed that he was interested in me, but of course we were never alone. If we had been, I probably would have been terrified. Even though I looked far older than fifteen, I had never dated a man, and sex was the furthest thing from my mind. I was scared to death even to think about it.

One day a friend of Rick's came in and told me that he'd been badly hurt in a hit-and-run car accident. I went to the hospital that afternoon. I introduced myself to his father and sister, then I sat in the small waiting room with them until the doctors had finished examining Rick. I felt awkward being there with his family, and I thought about leaving, but I just stood there holding the sandwich and the soda I had brought Rick from the restaurant. When a nurse wheeled him into the room, I was shocked. His head was grotesquely swollen. There were stitches all over his eyes and blood in his hair. He greeted me and gestured toward his father.

"When my father came in to see me today, he said, 'Hey, Rick, at least your eyes are looking better.' I knew my right eye was open, so I pointed to the left eye and I said, 'Yeah, Dad, I'll sure be glad when this one opens.' 'It is open,' my father answered. 'Then you'd better get a doctor over here real quick, 'cause I can't see shit out of it.' " Rick forced a laugh as he told the story. "They're taking me to Columbia Presbyterian Hospital in New York to find out if anything can be done," he added, "but they think I'm gonna be blind in one eye."

I said something useless like, "Oh, I'm sure it will be okay."

As we entered the noisy, poorly kept ward filled with sick men, Rick explained how the accident had happened. "I was on Route 35, hitchhiking," he said. "A police car coming from the other direction stopped to tell me not to hitchhike. The car behind it veered to get out of the cop's way and hit me. It flipped me up in the air and I came down on my head. The guy just kept going. The cops took off after him and caught him a couple of miles down the road. He turned out to be a kid who'd been drinking.''

After Rick's father and sister left, I wheeled him over to the sink and washed the blood out of his hair. Then I brushed it with my hairbrush and gently washed his injured face. We didn't talk much, but I could feel that there was something happening between us. I saw Rick close his eyes as I touched him. Not knowing what else to do and suddenly feeling shy, I gave him the sandwich and the soda and told him my father was picking me up downstairs. Then I leaned over to kiss him good-bye on the cheek, as I would any friend. Suddenly he grabbed me and kissed me. There was an intensity in his touch and kiss that I had never felt before. He held me as if he never wanted to let go. I was surprised and very embarrassed because all the men in the ward were watching and I had never really been kissed before. Just the same, I was thrilled. I remember thinking all the way home that I was going to marry him.

The next day he went to Columbia Presbyterian Hospital and learned that although the eye itself could be saved, the sight could not be restored; the optic nerve had been severed. Later that night he called. "I want to talk to you, Mary. I want to be near you," he said.

Right from the start, we loved being with each other. It quickly got to the point where he didn't want to take me home and I didn't want to go home. We were spending all our free time together. As soon as he was finished with work, he'd come to see me. He was even getting used to my huge family; that was very hard for him, because he'd grown up in a much quieter family that was only half the size of mine.

The third of four children and the youngest son of a policeman, Rick had learned early to follow the rules. He was a Cub Scout, a Boy Scout, and a Little League baseball player, a gentle boy who fished a lot and loved the sea. He was completely unprepared for the transition from a sheltered New Jersey shore community, where he had always lived, to active combat in the Mekong Delta.

As soon as he arrived in Vietnam, Rick was assigned to the 9th Division, a "bastard battalion" with no home base. The battalion was surrounded by farms, rice paddies, and small villages. The village kids would come to where the soldiers were camping and beg for things. There were about ten kids there one day, and when it turned out they were caught stealing from the troops, one of the guys who caught them picked up a concussion grenade and threw it into the group. The rice paddies were so dry and the ground was so hard that when the grenade went off, it made the dirt fly like shrapnel. It penetrated the children's skin and tore it apart. The children ran from the explosion, cut up and screaming in agony. That was the start of Rick's Vietnam tour.

In the months that followed, Rick traveled all over Vietnam. He spent his first six months with the 9th Division and his last seven months with the 101st. They were sent wherever there was a problem. At one point, in a jungle north of Hue, the old capital, Rick and five other men were setting up a landing zone so a chopper could bring in supplies. A big, blond, burly twenty-year-old from Kentucky was helping to clear the brush. Suddenly there was an explosion of gunfire. A rocket-propelled grenade blew half of the boy's face off. His mouth and chin were completely gone. The rest of the face was a shredded, unrecognizable blur. He was bleeding so profusely that it was hard to tell what was left.

A few days later the 101st Division lost fourteen other men to booby traps. All of them were in line behind Rick, who had somehow managed to step over fourteen traps. One of the men had both feet blown off. He ran on his stumps, screaming. Rick and the others had to tackle him, hold him down, bandage him, then shoot him full of morphine and stand by and hear him sing country-and-western songs as they waited for the medevac helicopter to come.

Rick survived Vietnam, but there was no time for him to adjust either at the beginning or the end of his tour of duty. When he found himself back in Ocean County, New Jersey, surrounded by his family and friends, he felt even more alone than he had felt in those snake-infested jungles and muddy foxholes. People tried to reach out. They patted him on the back and said they knew what he was going through. Rick wanted contact. He wanted the comfort of friends, but he couldn't connect.

He began spending more and more time in the bars and clubs that dotted the shoreline. He drank beer with the boys and listened to the laughter of the women. As the months passed, he became more and more aimless. Even the job he finally took as a truck driver for the asphalt company was just a way of marking time.

Ironically, Rick had survived Vietnam only to be injured on a New Jersey highway. When I visited Rick in the hospital the day after his accident, and he closed his eyes, for a moment his own swollen, injured face had become one with the bloody head of the soldier whose face had been blown off. But this time, just by chance, when he opened his eyes again, he was not alone. I was standing beside him, washing the blood from his face and hair, and for the first time, instead of feeling that he couldn't connect and that no one could help him or comfort him, he had seen me and he had reached out.

Of course, that day in the hospital, when I leaned over to kiss Rick good-bye and he grabbed me and held on, I knew none of this. Many years would pass before I could understand how perfectly Rick's need for a woman to help soothe the nightmare of Vietnam had meshed with my own deep longing to take care of someone. All either of us knew at the time was that we were in love. In less than six months, we were married.

Three weeks before our wedding, I realized that I was pregnant. At one level, my life was becoming exactly what I had always wanted it to be. I was, in my view, marrying my Prince Charming and having his baby. But, like most dreams with perfect endings, it was unrealistic. It was also happening much faster than I expected. I was still only sixteen years old and not really ready for marriage and motherhood.

I was scared. I didn't want to leave my family. I was afraid that I'd never see them again, that I'd lose them forever. I was taking on the role I had longed for, but I was also giving up the protection of living at home with my mother and father. For a time I felt I was losing my balance. One hundred and fifty people came to help celebrate my marriage to Rick, and all I could do was cry. I cried through the wedding vows, and I cried in the hotel at the shore where we spent our honeymoon.

Rick was gentle and kind. He didn't push me, then or ever. Even when I told him for months on end that all I wanted to do was be held, he comforted me and never forced himself on me. "I love you and that's all that matters," he would say soothingly.

During the pregnancy, I gained fifty pounds. I thought my body was becoming ugly and unrecognizable. I could hardly believe the changes. At sixteen, I was already looking back at my life with a sense that I had lost my youth forever.

For a time, during that first year, I withdrew from Rick almost completely. As I retreated more and more, so did he. Slowly, almost imperceptibly, each of us began to return to our earlier patterns. I was mindlessly playing house, cleaning, cooking, washing, and ironing, and Rick was spending more and more of his time alone, in those anonymous seaside bars, drinking beer.

# Chapter 9

# My Marriage to Rick

When it comes to love, to romantic love and sexual love, and married love, we have to learn again with difficulty how to let go of all kinds of expectations.

—Judith Viorst in *Necessary Losses*

**O**ne evening in October 1973, Rick left the bar after three or four beers and climbed into his truck. He was pulling a bulldozer and didn't notice that the chain had come loose. As he went around the circle on Route 70, he lost the bulldozer. When the police arrived, they smelled the beer on his breath, took him to the station house, and gave him an alcohol test. Rick was convicted of impaired driving and his license was suspended for six months. After that, I had to drive him back and forth to the paving company he was working for.

Rick was also working from late afternoon until dark, digging graves at a local cemetery. He was paid fifty dollars a week for digging graves, and ninety-eight dollars a week by the paving company. We were living at his mother's house. We had no health insurance to cover the pregnancy, and Rick was trying to earn enough to pay the $450 doctor's bill. I'd pick him up at one job and drive him to the next, then I'd sit there in the cemetery, reading a book and waiting for him.

When I was eight months pregnant, a piece of concrete flew into Rick's good eye. He walked around all day with the concrete in his eye. By evening it looked as if someone had taken a knife and cut slits in his eyeball. When we went to the doctor, he put drops in the eye to dilate the pupil, then put a patch over it in an effort to save it. Rick was now temporarily blind; he couldn't get in and out of the bathtub or even get dressed by himself.

At this point in the pregnancy, I was so large that I couldn't get behind the wheel of a car. My brother was helping Rick in and out of the tub, I was dressing him, and my mother was driving us places.

Rick couldn't stand the feeling of total helplessness and dependency. On July 6, he pulled the patch off his eye and announced that he was driving the car to a party. He was not supposed to get his license back until July 15. In an effort to keep him from driving, I took the keys and hid them in my bra. He was so mad that he left the house and walked to the party. I waited for hours, worrying that he was going to get drunk and get hurt and lose his eye.

Rick finally came in at three-thirty in the morning. He was still angry and very drunk. As soon as he walked into the house, my labor started. "I think I'm going to have the baby," I said. He staggered to the bed and passed out.

I called my mother and told her. She said, "Don't go to the hospital until your pains are three minutes apart."

I lay awake all that night, alone, beside my drunk husband and beside an empty cradle draped with yellow and white eyelet lace. I was stunned by the lonely intensity of the pain, and the realization that my lifetime dream of being a mother was about to come true.

The baby was perfect, with dark hair and full eyebrows. He was absolutely beautiful, just as I'd dreamed he'd be: eight pounds, one ounce; twenty-one inches long. I remember being almost overwhelmed by my instant connection with this helpless, fragile creature. But I also remember that I didn't want to hold him. I didn't know if I was afraid, or if it was because the pain of delivery was so intense. But I was beginning to understand that my life as a wife and mother was not going to be what I had always thought it would be.

When Ryan was three weeks old, Rick was fired. He had difficulty finding another job. Luckily, just when things were getting desperate, he received a $16,000 insurance settlement for the loss of his eye. It was more money than we'd ever seen in our lives, and we were delighted.

We moved out of Rick's mother's house and rented a house of our own. I bought white wicker furniture for the living room and decorated Ryan's room in lime green and yellow. In the weeks that followed, I created a doll's house, airy, light, clean, and safe. It looked and felt like the storybook house I had always dreamed of.

With the money that was left, Rick opened a landscaping business. He began contracting for a developer who was building condominiums in Bricktown. For a while, things were starting to improve. Rick bought a tractor, a trailer, and gardening implements. He invested thousands of dollars in shrubs for the condominiums.

Then, soon after Rick planted the shrubs, the developer went bankrupt and the water at the complex got turned off. Rick would go there and spend hours watering the shrubs with a fire hose. But it was a hot summer, and the shrubs burned up and died. We lost everything. We practically gave the tractor and truck away, just to survive.

To my amazement, I discovered I was pregnant again. There was no money at all, and no medical insurance for the new baby. We gave up the house, put the wicker furniture in storage, and moved in with my parents.

Once again, Rick began the long search for work. He finally landed a job driving a tractor-trailer back and forth to Georgia. It meant that he would be away for about five days at a time. We had never been apart before, and at this point in the pregnancy, I was so ill that some mornings I couldn't stand up. It was all I could do just to lie on the rug with Ryan beside me and pat him on the back. Of course, Ryan himself was only a baby, barely seventeen months old, when Tuesday was born.

The bad and good moments during that period, when both children were small, are inseparable for me. Even though life was not easy, my children were always a joy. Their gentleness, their love of life, their separate and distinct personalities, which here and there flowed into my own, continued to be my greatest source of pleasure. Even when I was awakened at night, again and again, from an already meager sleep, and even when there wasn't a moment of peace to go to the bathroom alone, I rarely felt deprived. Sometimes I waited for Rick to return from work and relieve me for an hour or two, but most of the time I had a sense that this is what women have always done, a sense that my destiny as a woman and a mother was finally being fulfilled.

Rick and I both wanted to be the best parents we

could. We believed that I should be at home with the babies, that it was important for their development. Even in the early 1970s, when life was a search for the job that would pay a few cents more an hour, I believed that it was better for us to do without than for me to be away from my children.

Later, when Ryan was in kindergarten and Tuesday was three, I began to work an evening shift two or three days a week at a rest home. During these evenings, I left the kids with Rick. I earned fifty or sixty dollars a week. It was just enough to buy shoes and clothing for the kids and a few extra things that we needed.

There were sixteen old ladies in the home. No one else wanted to be bothered with bathing them, so when I came on duty I'd always do it. Once I got slapped in the face by an old lady who didn't want me to wash her hair, but most of the women were gentle and sweet.

I especially remember Suzy and Paula. They were best friends, and they both lived in an absolute fantasy world. They walked arm-in-arm and thought they were nine years old. Suzy used to come up to me and say, "Does my mother know I'm here?"

"Yes, Suzy," I'd say, "your mother knows you're here. We called her, it's okay."

I used to sing to them; they enjoyed it. Sometimes they'd sing to me. Some of the women would stay up and watch the ten o'clock news with me. I got kind of lonely in that big old house when the ladies went to sleep, so I'd scrub the bathrooms and clean the linen closets. Then, toward morning, I'd crank up the heat so that it would be warm enough for them to get out of bed. The place was only half a block from my house, and sometimes I'd walk over with the kids during the day just to visit.

Over the years I took several other jobs that increased the family income without taking me away from the children during hours when they needed me. I worked as a waitress during the lunch rush, so that I was home when they left for school and home when they got back. Then there was Mrs. Shade. I took her to the hairdresser and grocery shopping, and cleaned her apartment. She had asked for my help so that her daughter wouldn't feel that she was a burden. One year I worked at a department store during November and December so that the kids would have extra Christmas presents. Tuesday was so excited by all the gifts under the tree that she woke up early on Christmas morning and unwrapped every single one, even Ryan's.

During those years, working was something I did to *supplement* the family's income. It wasn't until the late 1970s, when Rick's drinking began to interfere with his work, that I was faced with the need to support us.

Ever since his return from Vietnam, Rick had said that he found the casual atmosphere of the local bars relaxing. Having a couple of beers after work now and then seemed harmless enough, and for many years we both made excuses. Neither of us recognized Rick's drinking as a problem. But as time moved on, a pattern began to form. For us, the recognition that the pattern was a serious problem finally came when Rick destroyed our car, had his license suspended for the second time, and lost his job. Alcohol had clearly become a regular part of his life. Rick was stopping at the bars every day.

We had just finished restoring an old Oldsmobile Cutlass convertible. For a long time we had debated about whether to fix it up or not. We had finally decided that we loved the car so much, it was worth the money and the effort. We had the engine rebuilt, bought a new top, and repainted the car. It looked great and had everything we wanted.

On the day of the accident, Rick had taken the Cutlass to work at 5:00 A.M. and run a load of stones from the quarry back to the asphalt plant. By 7:00 A.M. he was back at the plant and ready to begin his regular job. He finished hauling asphalt at about seven o'clock that night and stopped at a bar with some friends. The combination of too little sleep, too much work, no dinner, and too many beers hit him on the way home. About a quarter-mile from our house, he fell asleep at the wheel of the Cutlass. He crashed into three telephone poles and destroyed the car.

When the police found him, they could tell he had been drinking. So once again they took him down to the police station and gave him an alcohol test. This time they locked him up. When I heard what had happened, I was so angry that I almost let him stay in jail overnight. Then I began to worry about whether he was hurt. I borrowed some money and a car, drove to the police station, bailed him out, and took him to the hospital. It turned out he had a broken nose and a concussion.

Rick's physical injuries were the least of his problems. He hadn't only crashed into three telephone poles, he had also finally been struck by the realization that his life was out of control. He wanted to run from alcohol, from his self-destructiveness, and from his own sense of failure. He felt terrible about what he had done to the car, to his job, and to us.

For Rick, the first part of trying to recover was standing alone, apart from me, on his own two feet and assuming full responsibility for himself. He left us and went to live at his mother's house in the nearby town of Manasquan. We had finally reached a point where we could no longer pretend to function as though nothing was wrong.

Without a driver's license, Rick was no longer employable as a truck driver. At that point, with no education and two children to support, I was in real trouble. Afraid that the children would literally go hungry, I applied for welfare. I hated the idea of accepting welfare, but I didn't know how I could find work that would allow me to be there for my children and still earn enough money to pay our rent, utilities, and food.

That was when I took a job as a barroom dancer. I never did anything that embarrassed my children or my husband, so there's not much to say. I was never nude or topless. In fact, I wore a one-piece bathing suit and stockings. The outfit was far less revealing than what most women wear on the beach today.

During the trial, the fact that I had worked as a go-go dancer was blown out of proportion. In truth, it was no big deal. My sister owned the bar and had offered me the job. Our family was in deep economic trouble, and I took it because it allowed us to survive.

During that period, I considered a divorce but I had two children and I still loved my husband. Even though Rick and I were separated, there wasn't a day that we didn't talk to each other.

While Rick was at his mother's, he began to attend AA meetings and to accept responsibility for his problem. A few months later he returned home. For a year he didn't drink at all. Then, just when it seemed we were back on our feet, he fell off the wagon.

I had dropped the kids off at my mother's for the evening and was waiting for Rick to come home so we could go out. He came in late. As soon as I saw him, I knew he was drunk. I was so disappointed and angry that I pushed him toward the door and yelled, "Get out, go and live with your mother!" He wouldn't leave. He just wanted to pass out and sleep it off. I kept telling him to go. When he refused to budge, I tried to pull him off the couch.

"Get away from me," he moaned angrily. And as he said it, he grabbed me and pushed me. I stumbled backward and fell across the vacuum cleaner. I was only slightly hurt by the fall, but I was deeply injured by his return to alcohol and his anger.

"If you don't leave, I'm calling the police!" I shouted. "I'm telling them I want you out of here."

"Go ahead, do whatever you want," he challenged.

I picked up the phone and called the police. When Rick saw that I was serious, he got up and staggered out. By the time the police arrived, I was sorry I had called them and sorry I had fought with Rick. As soon as I had filled out the report and answered their questions, I got into the car and drove straight to his mother's house.

"I'm sorry, Rick. I should have been more understanding. I know I overreacted," I said.

"I'm sorry too, Mary," he answered, reaching out to hold me. "I know it's my fault, and I'm going to try not to do it again."

Despite our differences, Rick and I had the kind of deep-running love that endured. For many years our love transcended poverty and alcohol; even in the raggedness of our deepest disappointments, I still saw Rick as my friend and protector. I no longer viewed love as the dreamlike, fairy-tale I had carried with me as a child. But I still desperately wanted to make our marriage work. That night was the first time that Rick and I viciously lashed out at each other. We knew that we had come closer to destroying our family than we had ever been. It frightened us because, at that point, neither of us was prepared to give up. Our marriage and family were still the things that we both treasured most.

During the first five years of the marriage, Rick never held a job for more than a year. Of course, that also meant there was never a paid vacation or any medical benefits. In the sixth year of our marriage, things began to improve. Rick got a job with the Marpal Disposal Company in Tinton Falls, New Jersey, a job that he kept until recently, when he moved to Florida. He worked six days a week, sometimes seven, collecting garbage.

During the trial, I heard people say, "You know, Rick doesn't really work, he's just a garbage man." These people simply don't know what it means to get up at 3:00 A.M., when the whole family is asleep, and go to work while it's still dark. They don't realize that it's hard, grueling, dirty work. I know, because I tried it.

Rick's boss had been looking for someone to help him, but the people he hired would work for one day, sometimes only half a day, and then walk off the job because it was so exhausting. Once when I came to pick Rick up, he kiddingly said to his boss, "You might as well give me Mary Beth. At least that way, we'll be going home with two paychecks."

"I'll do it," I volunteered enthusiastically, with no idea of what I was getting into.

"Go ahead, take her," the boss answered, smiling.

I'll never forget that day. It was a hot Saturday morning. The kids were visiting my mother. I got up at 3:00 A.M. and went to work. I started out carrying a barrel that felt as though it weighed 150 pounds. I had waitressed, so I was used to carrying heavy trays, but nothing like this barrel. We were doing back-door service, which meant that we went to the back of each house, got the garbage, and emptied it into a huge barrel. We were not only jumping over fences, we were carrying the barrels on our shoulders as we jumped.

I had never realized that Rick worked so hard. Just climbing in and out of the truck was a chore. I had to hoist myself up about six feet to get in, and often had to jump while the truck was still moving to get out. One person was supposed to collect the garbage and empty it into the barrels, while the other drove the truck. The barrels were so heavy that I decided to try driving the truck. I'm a good driver. I've never had an accident, and since I learned on a big car, I thought a garbage truck couldn't be much more difficult. But I couldn't do it. The power and weight behind it were something I had never experienced before. When I applied the brake, the truck just didn't want to stop. After ten frightening minutes, I turned the driving back over to Rick.

We pulled up to a TV shop. There must have been about ten console televisions on the curb. I had to pick them all up and throw them into the back of the hopper, where they would be crushed and pushed deeper in the truck. Suddenly the broken glass came shooting out. I was wearing pink shorts, and a pair of sneakers with white socks. Before I could jump out of the way, my legs were cut and spattered with blood. As Rick cleaned my legs, he told me that winter was not as bad as summer. "In winter it's always cold," he said, "but you work so hard that you stay warm. Because we live in a summer resort area, the garbage is also much lighter in the winter."

As we approached a fish market, Rick tried to prepare me. "Mary Beth," he said, "I think the worst part for you is going to be the maggots." Despite the warning, I was shocked when I opened up the garbage cans. There were so many maggots that they flowed like lava. I was supposed to empty them along with the trash into the barrels, then put the barrels on my shoulder. Rick was right, I didn't want those things near me. Looking slightly amused, Rick finally agreed to carry the barrels *and* do the driving.

Somehow we got through the day and finished half an hour ahead of schedule. All the way home, I vowed I'd never do it again. But the experience gave me a new level of respect for Rick's endurance. I'm still amazed that he adapted to that job and kept it for so many years. Of course, the steady income added a lot to our sense of security.

By the time Tuesday started kindergarten, we were settled in a house in Bricktown. My sister Beverly and her husband had originally bought it for themselves, but when they bought a business in another neighborhood, they decided to rent the house. They had had a string of tenants who had let the place get so run down that it was practically destroyed. When we moved in, the floors and bathroom were filthy. Kids had scribbled all over the walls, and the yard was an overgrown mess. We cleaned and scrubbed, painted and plastered. For the kitchen I chose wallpaper that had small green and pink hearts, and curtains that matched.

We had no den, so a round kitchen table with a black glass top became our family's gathering place. The living room was slightly more formal, with two pink and white sofas, separated by a small round table draped in the same material. There was also a cherry wall unit and a small cherry piano, which I bought when Tuesday decided she wanted to take piano lessons. The wooden floors were covered with area rugs and kept polished to a bright shine. It was a cozy, comfortable house with a small back porch and separate bedrooms for each of the children. I always felt that each child needed a room, not simply because one was a boy and one was a girl, but because right from the start they were very different kinds of children.

Ryan was always quiet and shy. As a toddler, he loved putting puzzles together. He'd sit for hours fitting together hundreds of little tiny pieces, no bigger than a dime. He also loved to draw. From the age of three, whenever Rick's brother, who was a draftsman, came to visit, Ryan would ask him to draw things—a football player, a truck, a tractor. Then he'd try to do it himself.

Grammar school was never easy for Ryan. He was happiest when he was alone. As far back as I can remember, he wanted to be a priest. To this day he doesn't like dirty jokes, and hates cigarettes and drugs. He was always more concerned with other people than with himself. If a child in school was picking on him, he wouldn't come home and tell me because he didn't want that child to get into trouble. Even though he's shy and sometimes awkward, he's a handsome boy, so much so that I sometimes look at him and say, "My God, is that my kid?" He's tall and so physically agile that we affectionately call him "the rubber-band man."

The Sterns' trial certifications and some of the press reports implied that Ryan was retarded. Nothing could be further from the truth. He recently scored 130 in a standard IQ test, and his teacher told me he was one of the smartest kids in his class. For some reason we don't fully understand, he's about two years behind in his reading. He makes up for it in other ways. He's excellent at math and he's a computer whiz. He gets complex games from the Sigma Entertainment System that most kids take weeks to figure out, but he masters them the first night.

When Bill Stern began sending certifications to the court, he told the judge that he didn't know why Ryan was living in Florida. Actually, Bill Stern and I had talked about it; the reason was not a secret. It was because the school system here didn't seem able to meet his needs. The school had wanted to keep him back because of his reading and his shyness. I felt very strongly that it would be a mistake to hold back a boy as bright as Ryan, especially since he was already big for his grade. Rather than have him repeat the year, I sent him to my mother's. I missed him very much and called him almost every day. He spent summers and vacations with us. We had never been apart before. As it turned out, he worked hard, stayed at the appropriate grade level, adapted well, and got all A's and B's. He returned home after finishing sixth grade.

For Tuesday, on the other hand, everything came easily. From the very beginning, she was an outgoing child who did a lot of things on her own. She walked at ten months and began toilet-training herself when she was fourteen months old. I didn't encourage her to do it. In fact, I figured it would be easier if she was still in diapers, because if she was toilet-trained, whenever we went someplace, we would have to run around looking for a toilet.

I also thought of her as my last baby, and I wasn't in a hurry to see her grow up. Nevertheless, she grew up very quickly. She was an excellent student, and she was always popular. She was also a star athlete in soccer by the time she was seven. On the other hand, she didn't have the same kind of quiet, introspective sensitivity that Ryan had. Tuesday got furious if someone violated something of hers; Ryan just got sad.

With Ryan in Florida and Tuesday in school all day, I found that for the first time in many years, I actually had time for myself. I also found that it wasn't all I'd hoped it would be. I had grown so used to living by the rhythm of my children's lives that I hardly knew what to do with the time. Now and then I would see an infant clinging to its mother and feel the old longing return. Being a mother was how I had always defined myself.

Having another child with Rick had been ruled out by a vasectomy he had had at the advice of our doctor shortly after Tuesday was born. At the time, we were young and poor, and two children seemed like all we'd ever be able to handle economically. Rather than risk another accident, my doctor had advised a more radical approach to birth control. I was considering having my tubes tied, but we had heard that the procedure was more dangerous than a vasectomy.

Although I didn't fully understand it, I found that I missed not being needed from morning until night. I'd spent my whole life caring for, listening to, and nurturing other people. Then I saw the ad in the *Asbury Park Press* asking for women to help infertile couples have babies. I responded immediately. In many ways, surrogacy seemed like the ideal solution. It was, I reasoned, a way for me to help someone less fortunate, by doing what I was born to do. It was then, in March of 1984, that I called the Infertility Center and was sent an application.

Before I met the Sterns, I tried for eight months to conceive a child for another couple. The woman had undergone a hysterectomy, but no one knew that the husband had virtually no sperm count. Finally, when I failed to become pregnant, the Infertility Center performed some basic tests. When I realized what the problem was, I was so discouraged and angered by the Center's incompetence that I considered giving up the whole idea.

That was when I heard from Bill Stern. He called me one evening after getting my number from the Infertility Center, introduced himself over the phone, and asked if I'd like to have his baby.

"Is your wife there? I'd like to speak to her," I said.

"I think it's better if you don't right now," he answered. We agreed that all four of us would meet for dinner at Victoria Station, a restaurant in New Brunswick, which was halfway between our houses.

On the night of our meeting, it was snowing so hard that we almost canceled. Rick and I both noticed that the Sterns were very quiet. But I was so excited about having a baby and so eager to like them that I told myself they were probably just nervous. We agreed to move forward.

A few days later, a contract arrived from the Infertility Center. I signed it at my kitchen table. Ten days after that, I was artificially inseminated with Bill Stern's sperm for the first time. In the months that followed, Bill and I would meet at the Thomas Edison exit on the New Jersey Turnpike and drive to the Infertility Center in New York together. Bill was always nervous about getting to the city on time. If we were late, he would take his gloves and cover the clock with them so that he wouldn't look at the time. Then he would drive like a maniac.

The arrangement seemed odd and unnatural. We were two strangers who were attempting to achieve the most intimate human connection possible without ever touching each other. We used to sit there together in all those hours of traffic with little or nothing to say.

When we finally got to the Center, Bill would go into a small private room and come out a few minutes later, carrying his sperm. Then I would go into another private room and be inseminated while he waited outside. After that, we'd start the long drive back.

A couple of times I said to him, "Boy, Bill, this is a ridiculous process." Once I asked him why he and Betsy had chosen to do it.

"It's a legacy to my mother," he answered.

"Why can't Betsy have a child?" I ventured.

When Bill didn't answer, I found myself searching through my own family experiences for an explanation. I told him that my sister was unable to become pregnant.

"If Betsy ever became pregnant, she'd probably die," Bill finally said.

"What do you mean?" I asked.

"She would probably die," he repeated emphatically, and then fell silent without elaborating. Whatever it is, I said to myself, ashamed for broaching the subject, it must be *very* serious.

During the seven months that I was regularly inseminated with Bill Stern's sperm, we remained intimate strangers. I learned very little about the man whose child I would bear. Perhaps it was because what I'd assumed was a friendship was only a financial arrangement to him.

Looking back now, I find it difficult to understand how a man with a Ph.D. in biochemistry and a woman with a Ph.D. in human genetics, as well as an M.D., could literally select me from a picture book without exploring the critical genetic role that I would play in the baby's life and without even reading my psychological evaluation. Yet, according to Betsy Stern, they never asked for the psychologist's report that warned that I might not be able to part with the baby.

I now believe that even if Betsy had read the report, I would have remained incomprehensible to her. We were such different kinds of women. Betsy valued her career with the same intensity that I valued motherhood. She was a twenty-nine-year-old Ph.D. the year she married Bill Stern. At the time of their marriage, I was only eighteen, but I was already the mother of two children. After finishing her Ph.D., Betsy decided to go to medical school and wait another seven years before considering pregnancy. By then she was thirty-six, and had a mild, self-diagnosed case of multiple sclerosis.

In all those months it never occurred to me that Betsy could actually have given birth to a child. All the women I knew who really wanted children were willing to go to almost any extreme, including great personal risk, to have a baby. I had felt so strong a desire to experience pregnancy that it would have been hard for me to comprehend that Betsy or any other woman might not want to.

Each day, month after month, I took my temperature with a basal thermometer. Becoming pregnant was the main focus of my life. After each insemination I would lie on the table for forty-five minutes with my legs as high as I could get them. I practically stood on my head, because the doctor had told me it would increase the possibility of conception. It got to the point where I wouldn't clean or cook or do anything on the days that I was inseminated,

AP

Noel Keane, whose Infertility Center arranged the surrogacy contract between the Sterns and me. For each deal Keane arranged, he received a nonrefundable $10,000 fee. The year I was pregnant with Sara, Noel Keane publicly claimed he had arranged three hundred births, presumably grossing $3,000,000.

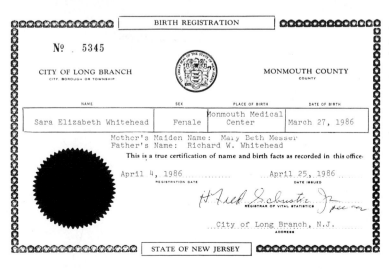

On her birth certificate, my daughter was identified as "Sara," the name Rick and I had chosen for her. Later, the court referred to her as "Baby M," reflecting the Sterns' choice of "Melissa." The difference between the name on the birth certificate and the name on the court order demanding that I surrender my baby confused the police.

Al Paglione/The Bergen Record

My daughter Tuesday and I have always been close. A very perceptive and mature child, Tuesday was the first to recognize that surrogacy was wrong. "I wish we could keep the baby," she confided late in my pregnancy. "She will never forgive you if you give her up."

The Bergen Record

My first encounter with Judge Harvey Sorkow was after the Sterns had seized Sara while I was in an intensive care unit with a severe kidney infection. I was naively hopeful and eager for a chance to explain what had happened. But the hostile courtroom atmosphere was apparent at once. "My God," I cried, "they're stealing my baby and they're getting away with it."

UPI

My husband Rick, Tuesday, and me after the hearing in which the Sterns were awarded temporary custody of "Baby M." The decision seemed to be based on one expert's certification that because Sara had been with the Sterns for six weeks, they should continue to have custody. Apparently, the expert ignored the fact that I had been breast-feeding Sara for four months before she was taken away from me.

Lorraine Abraham (the *guardian ad litem*), me, and my attorney Alan Grosman. After the Sterns had been awarded temporary custody, I was allowed to visit Sarah only once a week at the Conklin Center, a home for delinquent children. During one visit, Abraham shocked me by asking, "Tell me, Mary Beth, who's going to play your part in the movie?"

As the trial dragged on, I began to lose confidence that Sara would ever be able to come home. Sometimes I felt as if the whole horrible struggle was crushing my spirit.

On Christmas Eve, Rick, Tuesday, my son Ryan, and I were allowed to visit Sara, the first time Rick and the children were able to see her since she was seized in July. We brought presents with us. My choice of panda bears would later be criticized by one of the expert witnesses as being inappropriate for a nine-month-old infant. The expert thought that pots and pans and spoons would have been "more characteristic of the needs of the baby."

March 31, 1987. Bill and Betsy Stern express their relief when they are awarded permanent custody by Judge Harvey Sorkow. Their attorney Gary Skoloff looks on. My parental rights were terminated and Judge Sorkow conducted an instant adoption ceremony in his chambers.

In his ruling, Judge Sorkow branded me "manipulative, impulsive, and exploitative . . . a woman without empathy." My legal counsel described the judge's ruling as "so terrible that it's wonderful," explaining that the higher courts would be likely to agree to hear our case. At a press conference the day after the ruling, I vowed to continue my fight for my baby and noted that there could "never be a court-appointed termination of my love for Sara."

On April 10, 1987, the New Jersey Supreme Court reinstated my visitation rights pending appeal of the lower court decision. Although Rick and I were ecstatic about this news, the stress of the long court battle was starting to pull us apart.

No words could express the joy and relief I felt when the New Jersey Supreme Court released its decision on February 3, 1988, restoring my parental rights. Here I am happily embracing my attorney Harold Cassidy. It would be several days before I had time to read the eloquent ninety-five-page opinion in its entirety. When I read it, I was astounded by how profoundly the seven justices had perceived both my suffering and that of the Sterns.

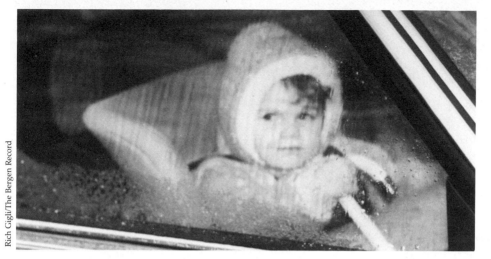

Melissa, at almost one year of age, in the Sterns' car after a visit with me at the Conklin Center.

My attorney Joel Siegel and my new husband, Dean Gould, lent moral support during the visitation hearing that took place after the New Jersey Supreme Court ruling. Although it was still difficult to accept, I had by now become resigned to the fact that my daughter would not be living with me full-time. I would soon be blessed with a new baby, Austin, and I was grateful that I would still be able to play a role in Melissa's life.

On April 7, 1988, Judge Birger Sween increased the length of my weekly visits with Melissa, including future overnight visits and two-week summer vacations. Sween noted that Melissa and I "have the right to develop [our] own special relationship." Here, on April 12, 1988, Bill delivers Melissa to the Conklin Center for our first unsupervised visit . . . and I am finally able, after almost two years of being apart, to bring Melissa home.

because I didn't want anything to reduce my chances of becoming pregnant.

Then, finally, after seven months of trying to conceive with Bill's sperm, my normally prompt period was late. I tested my urine with a pregnancy test kit. When the stick turned blue, I ran to the phone and called Betsy. "I am pregnant," I announced joyfully.

"Now wait a minute, Mary Beth," she said. "I don't believe that. Let's not take any chances. Go and get a blood test."

"Oh, Betsy, don't be a gloom-doom," I answered, laughing.

Just the same, that afternoon, I drove to Planned Parenthood in Red Bank and got the blood test. It came back positive. That night, as a surprise for Bill, Betsy decorated their bathroom with signs that said "SHE'S pregnant."

The excitement and fulfillment that I felt during those early months of pregnancy were so strong and deep that I barely stopped to wonder what it all meant. I remember that when Sara began kicking, Rick and I would sometimes lie in bed together, feeling the life within me and marveling at how strong the baby's kick was. If there was a silent awareness of what was to come, we were both suppressing it.

Bill and Betsy had gone off to Europe for a vacation. When they returned, they said they wanted me to have an amniocentesis performed. My doctor said that I didn't need it, but they insisted, saying that they didn't want a baby with a handicap, they wanted a "perfect" baby.

I drove to the hospital by myself. Betsy and Bill met me there. I didn't want to be there, and I think it was the beginning of the rift that grew between us. I was very nervous, and the baby's heartbeat became irregular, indicating that she, too, was in distress as they drew the fluid out of me. I began to get the feeling that we were playing God, tampering with nature in a way that made me very uncomfortable. When I got home I wanted to explain my feelings to Rick, but I still couldn't really grasp them. "You know," I said, struggling inarticulately with the concept that had not yet crystallized, "it may be their baby, but it's still my body and something we're doing just doesn't seem right."

In the fifth month, I developed a huge black and blue mark on the inside of my thigh. It was painful, burning, and raised. The doctor sat me down. "Mary Beth," he said, "you have phlebitis. It's an inflammation of the veins that can form a blood clot that can go to the heart, so don't mess around with it." For two weeks I stayed in bed. Rick did the laundry and every evening my sister-in-law, Sherri, brought dinner over. Soon, after I recovered from the phlebitis, I began to develop another symptom.

It started with headaches. Next my face would become burning hot. Then, one morning, as I was sitting at the kitchen table drinking a cup of coffee, blood began to pour out of my nose. I never told Betsy about the nosebleeds, even though they occurred several times, because a week earlier, when I had mentioned that my blood pressure was up, she had said, "Mary Beth, I want you in bed. You're not to get up." By that time, I felt she was so overbearing that I simply stopped communicating.

A few days later, an insurance agent called and told me the Sterns were taking out a $100,000 life insurance policy for me. He said it was part of the contract and that Rick would be the beneficiary. He just needed to know my age and if I had ever had a heart problem or kidney disease. In fact the Center did routinely recommend that couples buy insurance in order to prevent a lawsuit if the surrogate mother died in childbirth. But I was so rattled by my medical problems that I reacted by thinking, Oh my God, I've gained fifty-five pounds and have phlebitis and high blood pressure. They must know I'm not going to make it.

The next afternoon I was feeling slightly better and was on my way to a soccer game with Tuesday when she said, "Hurry up, Mom, you're walking like an old lady."

"I can't help it, Tuesday," I said. "Someday you'll have a baby, then you'll know what it feels like."

"No, I won't," she answered. "I'm going to hire someone like you to do it for me."

I hated hearing Tuesday say that. She and I had always been very close, and I knew she was at a vulnerable stage where she often modeled her behavior on mine. Suddenly I realized that this pregnancy, which I had always thought was so altruistic, was actually reinforcing the wrong values.

"I wish we could keep her, Mom. I'd like to have a sister."

Ever since the amniocentesis, we had known it was going to be a girl, and that knowledge had heightened Tuesday's sense of closeness with the unborn baby.

"If we kept her, it would hurt Betsy and Bill," I said matter-of-factly.

"Well, I'd be sorry for them," she responded, "but it would be better for the baby, Mom," she continued, her voice trembling and her eyes filling with tears. "She will never forgive you if you give her up, and if she grows up and finds out that you *sold* her, she will hate you." We walked the rest of the way to the soccer game in silence. I knew that, despite her age, my ten-year-old daughter had understood the truth more clearly than I had. I would never forget the look on her face or the words she had spoken.

After that, I often lay awake at night, thinking about what was going to happen when the baby was born. I still couldn't fully grasp what it was going to be like to part with my daughter.

One afternoon at the beginning of my ninth month, I went shopping with my mother and bought Sara an outfit to wear home from the hospital. As I left the store, I became painfully aware that I missed preparing for the baby's homecoming. I longed to wash and iron and fold and make ready all those little clothes.

That night, Betsy called and said she had gone out and bought the baby some clothing. My head was spinning. My God, I thought dumbly, this woman is planning to take *my* baby home with her. That was when I should have stood my ground and said, "Betsy, don't buy anything else, because I can't do it. I can't part with her. I can't give her to you." But I was so afraid of hurting her, and so confused by my own growing sense of attachment to this unborn baby, that I said nothing.

# Chapter 10

# Pretrial Hearings

By four months, babies become increasingly wary of
whoever is *not* mother, and try to avoid close contact with
that outside person . . . even a familiar "other" may create
anxiety. The baby will . . . cry relentlessly if he is picked up
by a "familiar" stranger. Not until his mother takes him back
will he stop crying. . . . [It is] a time when the child's
awareness of differences and their importance is at a new
peak.

—T. Berry Brazelton, M.D., in
*To Listen to a Child*

**N**ow, on August 13, al-
most five months later, as Tuesday and I boarded the
plane that would take us from Florida back to New Jersey,
I had a sudden image of Sara screaming in fear as she was
whisked from the police station to an airplane by the
Sterns. All during the trip, I kept trying to understand Bill
and Betsy's reasoning. They knew that by four and a half
months, Sara, like all babies, was deeply attached to her
mother and cried whenever I was out of sight. I simply
couldn't imagine how they could have ripped a nursing
baby from my breast without weaning her and placed her
in an unfamiliar house, surrounded by strangers.

As a pediatrician, Betsy must have realized that children of this age actually form a mental image of their missing mother and search frantically for her. Then, if the mother does not return, they grieve for her as adults grieve for people who have died. Betsy and Bill must also have known that many experts believe that the damage done to a child by this kind of sudden loss is likely to be permanent.

Rick's sister and brother-in-law picked us up at Newark Airport. We drove directly to the Bergen County Courthouse in Hackensack, New Jersey, where I was to meet Judge Harvey Sorkow for the first time. After greeting my attorney, Alan Grosman, I entered the judge's courtroom. I looked at the fifty-seven-year-old man who was to determine the fate of my daughter. I knew he was the same judge who had issued the May 5 order to seize Sara, as well as the order for my arrest. Still, I was naïvely hopeful and eager for a chance to explain what had happened. But Judge Sorkow looked right past me and locked his cold gaze on a cameraman filming us as we walked into the courtroom.

"Under no circumstances will that footage appear anyplace," he snapped. "I don't want that on film. There are no cameras allowed in the courtroom."

"Yes, Your Honor. My intention wasn't to shoot in the courtroom but to get the woman walking through the door," the cameraman said, pointing at me.

"I don't want that on the film," Sorkow ordered.

"I'll tell that to my reporter, Your Honor," the cameraman answered politely as he retreated from the doorway of the courtroom.

"All right," Sorkow said, turning his attention first to Gary Skoloff, the bearded, middle-aged attorney who represented the Sterns, then to Alan Grosman. He asked them what their respective positions would be on his own motion to appoint a guardian *ad litem* to represent the baby. "I favor it, Your Honor," Alan Grosman said.

"I object," Gary Skoloff countered. "It would be unnecessary. Nothing would be accomplished by it."

Sorkow, who seemed to have made up his mind ahead of time, then announced that he was appointing Lorraine A. Abraham as guardian *ad litem*.

We couldn't have been in the courtroom for more than five minutes when suddenly, before I had a chance to speak or realize what was happening, the judge dismissed us and walked out of the courtroom. He never even addressed the issue of when I would see Sara.

I returned home, depressed and exhausted, to find that my front door had been sealed because of the writ of attachment the judge had placed on my house. I still had criminal charges pending against me for taking Sara to Florida. I knew I was facing a possible eighteen-month jail term and a $15,000 fine on the charge of interference with custody. I thought that if I went into my house, even to sleep, I might be arrested, so Tuesday and I went to my brother's house.

As it turned out, since the Sterns now had custody of Sara, there was absolutely no legal ground for attaching my property. Even though this was clear to everyone involved, it took an additional three weeks for Judge Sorkow to respond to an order that Bob Arenstein, co-counsel to Alan Grosman, presented. During that period we remained homeless without explanation or apology.

Rick had no job, and of course we had no money. He was afraid to approach his old boss because he had left without giving notice. After months of looking for a new job, Rick accidentally bumped into his old boss, who immediately offered to take him back—but at the bottom of the pay scale. The salary would be only half of what Rick had been making. When I checked with the union, they told me the company didn't have the right to do that. But Rick was so glad to have a job again that he had already accepted the offer. After a while, Rick did get back up to scale.

On August 21, I returned to court. It had been almost a month since I had seen Sara. I was still pumping my breasts every two or three hours and pouring the milk down the drain. I had high hopes for that day. There was *finally* supposed to be a pretrial hearing to determine who should have temporary custody of Sara. Alan Grosman had assured me that our chances were good, since it was clearly in an infant's best interest to be with its natural mother. He also said that because vasectomies had sometimes been known to fail, Rick might be the father. There was, he added, a possibility that the Infertility Center had slipped up and given me the sperm of another donor. For those reasons, Grosman said he would request that blood tests be performed to determine Sara's paternity.

As soon as we came into the courtroom, I saw Lorraine Abraham, the dark-haired, middle-aged, newly appointed guardian for Sara. She was nodding her head and laughing as she talked to the judge.

First, Judge Sorkow announced that arguments would be heard on my motion for change in custody. Then he immediately added that "an alternative to a change of custody would be visitation." After a few minutes he turned his attention to the Florida paternity order, which had been delivered by the Sterns' attorneys to Alan Grosman for the first time as he walked into the courtroom. Grosman showed the Florida documents to me. I told him that Rick and I did not know about the proceedings and had never signed any paternity papers.

"Do you intend to recognize the Florida paternity order?" Grosman asked, jumping up from his seat. "It's a fraud. The judgment is invalid."

"This is a certified copy of a judgment of a sister state," the judge answered, "and I am obliged to give full faith and credit to that order. The only way you can attack a foreign judgment is jurisdictionally."

"I can attack it for fraud," Grosman said. "Fraud vitiates everything. . . . I'm saying the judgment is invalid."

They argued for several minutes and then the judge said, "It's your burden to convince the court that it should be successfully set aside. I would like to have the brief on my desk on Wednesday, September third, and I will schedule a hearing on the issue of this foreign judgment on September tenth, a week thereafter." His eyes swept the courtroom. "All circumstances will remain status quo until that date," he added.

"What circumstances?" Grosman asked, jumping up from his seat again.

"Location, presence of the child, all situations, status quo, that's the order," the judge answered. Suddenly, Alan Grosman realized that the fraudulent paternity order was now going to delay the temporary custody hearing and even the question of visitation with Sara for another three weeks. As he rose to object, Judge Sorkow interrupted him.

"I will tell you straight out," Sorkow growled, glancing in my direction, "your client is lying or telling the truth. Right now, it looks like there is a severe question about credibility. And I am not going to make any changes until all these preliminary matters are resolved." What he seemed to be referring to was the fact that the fraudulent document in the Florida paternity proceeding, which Rick and I never saw or signed, stated that Rick and I had not been sleeping together when Sara was conceived, while the papers we had submitted to Judge Sorkow truthfully said that we had been together at that time.

"The child, in my opinion, is being irrefutably harmed by the courts," Grosman shouted.

"Mr. Grosman," the judge interrupted, "I have made my order, and I will not have any more from you!"

I stood at the back of the courtroom, clutching Rick's hand. I could hardly believe what was happening. When Sorkow dismissed us, I walked into the hallway with my head spinning. "My God," I said when I saw my sister-in-law standing in the crowd, "they're stealing my baby and they're getting away with it."

The confusion outside the courtroom mirrored the turmoil in my head. More than a hundred reporters, photographers, and TV people were pushing, shoving, and practically knocking each other down. They all wanted to get to me, but at that moment the only thing I wanted was to be left alone. Tuesday was standing beside me, crying, frightened by the aggressiveness of the press. Alan Grosman was so furious that he had run outside cursing.

"Hey, this is a family newspaper," one reporter yelled.

"Well, I'm angry," Grosman responded. "This is just another delaying tactic. Florida has nothing to do with this proceeding. My client came back here willingly, with criminal charges pending against her. She wants to *see* her baby. Her rights are being violated, with the potential for irreparable damage to her."

Five days later, on August 26, Ryan, Tuesday, Rick, and I reported to Lorraine Abraham's office for a mandatory family interview. She started by asking me standard questions about my brothers and sisters. Then she looked up at me and asked, "Why are you talking to the *press*, Mary Beth?"

"Because some day, when Sara is old enough to understand, I want her to know that I tried," I answered.

"No, no," she responded impatiently, "that's not the real reason. Dig deeper, dig deeper." My eyes filled with tears. "Save your tears for television," she snapped, "because you won't get any sympathy here."

She continued to hammer away at me, asking for reasons and then rejecting each one until I finally realized that she wasn't going to stop and she wasn't going to like any of my answers. I began to get angry and I said, "Because I think the judge is against me. Because they're stealing my baby and I want to prevent it. And the only way I know how is to let the press know and to hope that maybe somebody out there will be able to stop it."

The next day, at Lorraine Abraham's request, Judge Harvey Sorkow's office issued a gag order, restraining me from talking to the press.

Despite my growing sense of despair, I still knew little about Harvey Sorkow, Gary Skoloff, or Lorraine Abraham. I did not yet realize that Lorraine Abraham was an old personal friend, hand-picked by Judge Sorkow. Nor did I know, until Lorraine Abraham made it clear to the

*Bergen Record* in Hackensack, that she had already decided that the Sterns might be better able to care for Sara because they had more income and education. Abraham was harshly criticized in the press by several of her peers for making such a comment publicly.

Later I learned that it was not the first time she had been considered inappropriately outspoken. Abraham had been a Teaneck, New Jersey, municipal judge from 1981 to 1985, until police and attorneys claimed that she made indiscreet and insulting remarks from the bench. At that time, the Teaneck Township Council held a closed-door meeting with her about the complaints. Press reports confirmed that she resigned soon after she was told that she would have trouble being reappointed.

I *had* noticed from the start that she and the Sterns seemed unusually friendly and that Judge Sorkow fiercely defended her judgment whenever it was questioned. He frequently referred to Lorraine Abraham as "an arm of the court, whose function is to help the court determine what's going on out there."

As the months passed, I also learned that Judge Sorkow and Gary Skoloff were longtime colleagues who both specialized in the same area of family law, and that Sorkow often referred to the three-volume textbook on the subject that Gary Skoloff had written.

Now, in September of 1986, only one thing had occurred that *appeared* to be in my favor. The Florida paternity order had been vacated by a Florida court, and Judge Harvey Sorkow now agreed that it was invalid.

When we returned to court on September 10 for yet another pretrial temporary custody hearing, Alan Grosman once again raised the subject of the Florida order. This time Judge Sorkow waved his arm, impatiently indicating that he didn't want to discuss it, and mumbled, "That's all moot now."

"It's not *quite* moot, Your Honor," Grosman responded, pointing out that Bill Stern had obtained the May 5 order that allowed police to storm my house, take my nursing infant without notice, and deliver her to him, by using the invalid paternity order.

"This court was prevailed upon and deceived by Mr. Stern and his agents in the Infertility Center in New York," Grosman said. "And it was asked to do a very extreme thing: take a baby from her mother without any prior notice. . . . No other state *ever* upheld such a contract without giving the natural mother the right to reconsider her decision and keep her baby. . . . Mr. Stern came into this court and *lied* to you, Judge," Grosman added, looking almost incredulous.

"I know what you're saying," Sorkow responded. "I know that you are alleging fraud. . . . I understand further that other states have not abided by the contract . . . but that doesn't in any way bind *this* state." With that, Sorkow dismissed Grosman's entire argument.

When the subject turned to Sara's paternity, Judge Sorkow asked what conclusion Grosman would draw if Rick's blood test revealed that he was not Sara's father.

"None, Your Honor," Grosman answered, "because Mrs. Whitehead could have been inseminated with some other sperm donor's sperm."

Judge Sorkow stared at me, then looked back at Alan Grosman. "Is she prepared to testify that she *slept* with other men . . . ?" the judge roared.

"You didn't hear me, Your Honor," Grosman said, confused by the jump in Sorkow's reasoning.

"I heard you," Sorkow repeated indignantly. "Is she

prepared," he repeated, "to testify that she *slept* with other men . . . ?"

"No, no, she's not," Grosman replied quickly.

"Excuse me, excuse me, excuse me," the judge said, his voice rising to a crescendo. "You know, Mr. Grosman, I should like to have a sense of order to our hearing, and I don't like to be continually interrupted."

"Well, why does Your Honor mention the prospect—"

"May I finish?" the judge shouted.

"—of adultery?" Grosman stammered.

"You're the one that said that, I didn't," the judge retorted.

"A sperm donor from a sperm bank," Grosman managed incredulously, practically choking on the words.

"If you would not interrupt me, I would finish my thought and you would be able to relax in your seat," Sorkow said. "I asked if Mrs. Whitehead is prepared to testify (a) that she went to bed with others, *or* (b) that she was inseminated in some other fashion by others? Now, had I not been interrupted, I would have finished that and all of your colloquy would have been unnecessary. Thank you, Mr. Grosman.

"Now, Mr. Grosman . . . talk to me about Baby M," Sorkow continued, emphasizing the letter *M*, which he had personally assigned to the case, a letter that clearly stood for the name Melissa, which the Sterns had given the baby. "Talk to me about the child and the mother."

Alan Grosman tried every approach. First he spoke of my competence as a mother and of the terrible mistake I had made in leaving the jurisdiction. Then he turned to my love for the baby and his belief that the Sterns would never have let her go home with me if they had *actually* believed, as they now claimed, that I was suicidal. Not only was Sorkow not moved by the plea, he was angered.

"Mr. Grosman," Sorkow said, "I'm going to tell you once and I'm not going to tell you anymore, I want to hear your argument as to why Baby M should be *returned* to her mother."

Alan Grosman shook his head silently. Sara's return was precisely what he *was* addressing. He took a deep breath and tried again.

"Your Honor," he said as calmly as he could. "Baby M should be returned to her mother because her mother is the most fit person to have primary custody of the child at this time of her life. . . . I have submitted to the court the certification of a very prominent child psychiatrist on the general issue, Dr. Alan M. Levy, a professor of clinical psychiatry at Columbia College of Physicians and Surgeons. He says . . . that it's in the . . . best interest of this child to spend more time with the mother, particularly if she is nursing the child."

As soon as Alan Grosman finished, Judge Sorkow asked Lorraine Abraham to speak. Abraham had independently sought another expert's advice. "Dr. Solnit's certification is before the court," she said, "and he feels that since the baby has already been with the Sterns for six weeks, she should stay there."

"But, Judge," Alan Grosman gasped, "this court *put off* the hearing for weeks . . . and the guardian said on the record, on August twenty-first, that she wasn't going to take *any* position about what should be done at this time."

"At *that* time," the judge corrected.

"And now she's champion of keeping the child with the Sterns?" Grosman asked pointedly.

"In the absence of showing that there is an *enormous*

detriment to this child," Lorraine Abraham responded, ". . . that it is being *abused* . . . based on Dr. Solnit's representation, I would have to recommend it remain where it is."

"Dr. Solnit's certification ought to be totally discredited and rejected by the court," Grosman countered, "because in paragraph six, Dr. Solnit says, 'I am familiar with the facts of this case *as reported in the press*' . . . and no one knows better than Your Honor how distorted the facts in the press are."

Alan Grosman was referring to Judge Sorkow's ruling that no personal material on either the Stern family or my family be released. Yet, right after his own ruling, the judge himself released copies of Bill Stern's most damaging, unproven certifications about me to the press. The next day, after the statements appeared in print, Sorkow said, "Oh my, that was an accident. Please tell Mrs. Whitehead that I am sorry."

"Your Honor," Grosman now said, referring to the error, "if he got the facts from, say, *The New York Times*, they contained some of the defamatory allegations that you tried *not* to have released."

Sorkow nodded and called for a recess.

When the court reassembled, Judge Sorkow lost no time in issuing his ruling. He said that the baby would remain with the Sterns.

I would be allowed two one-hour visits a week, "strictly supervised under constant surveillance . . . in a sequestered, supervised setting to prevent flight or harm." Several weeks later, at Grosman's request, Judge Sorkow increased these to two two-hour visits a week.

The press would not be allowed full access to the upcoming trial and hearings except—and this might be the most telling of all for future hearings—on the "termination" of my parental rights and "adoption proceedings" by Betsy Stern.

Almost four months before the trial began and more than six months before he issued his formal opinion, I felt certain that Judge Harvey Sorkow had *already* made up his mind.

# Chapter 11

# The Conklin Center

Take a child from his mother and put him with strangers in a strange place and he will scream, he will weep, he will thrash about, he will eagerly, desperately, search for his missing mother. He will protest because he has hope. Then after a while, when she doesn't come . . . and doesn't come . . . protest will turn to despair, to a state of muted, low-key yearning that may harbor an unutterable sorrow. . . . Furthermore, as early as six months old he may become, nor merely weepy and sad, but gravely depressed.

—Judith Viorst in *Necessary Losses*

**O**n September 27, 1986, I arrived at the Conklin Center, a facility for delinquent children, in a police car, accompanied by two sheriffs. Sara came with two guards and Lorraine Abraham. They carried her in and handed her to me. She looked the same, and yet she looked so different that I barely knew her. She seemed dazed, emotionally wounded. Two months earlier, at only four months of age, she had walked in her walker with so much energy, excitement, and enthusiasm that I could hardly get her to slow down. Now, at six months, she seemed barely able to support her own body weight. She was listless and apathetic. The sparkle and energy that had characterized her were completely gone.

I held her in my arms and rocked her, but all she would do was sob. "Oh, my poor baby," I whispered, wiping the tears from her eyes, "what have they done to you?" All I could think of was what she must have gone through in those five weeks.

"Don't upset her, Mary Beth," Lorraine Abraham said. I looked up at Lorraine Abraham for a minute, then I looked past her, at the dirty walls, the metal chairs, and the hallway monitored by four guards. I felt as if I were in prison with my own baby daughter. I kissed Sara and stroked her hair, but still she wouldn't stop crying. I wanted to calm her and let her know who I was.

As I rocked her in my arms, I began to sing to her. During the four months that she had been with me, I had often sung to her when I gave her a bath, when I changed her on the bed, and when I nursed her. I thought that perhaps it would jar her memory if I sang to her now. I began tentatively, humming at first, then singing quietly.

"I'll never find another girl like you . . . for happy endings it takes two . . . Sara, Sara . . . storms are brewing in your eyes . . . Sara, Sara . . . no time is a good time for good-byes."

The sound of my voice seemed to awaken something in her. Gradually she stopped crying and began to root for my breast. I could feel my milk rush in. Within a minute or two, she was clawing at my chest and pulling at my shirt. I thought of all the weeks that I had pumped my breasts, just waiting for this moment. I looked up at Lorraine Abraham and asked, "May I nurse her?"

"No," she said firmly.

"But why not?" I said. "She remembers the nursing and she wants to."

"Because I said so," Lorraine Abraham answered.

Not knowing what else to do, I held Sara against my

breast as if I were nursing her, and kept singing to her and rocking her. Finally, with her lips still making sucking motions against my milk-stained shirt, she fell asleep in my arms.

"What are you doing over there?" Lorraine Abraham asked when Sara grew quiet.

"Nothing," I answered sadly as I stroked Sara's hair.

Then Lorraine Abraham drew her chair closer and said, "Tell me, Mary Beth, who's going to play your part in the movie?"

I was completely astonished.

"My hairdresser and I have been talking about it," she continued, "and we thought Veronica Hamel, from 'Hill Street Blues,' should play me. And we thought that Walter Matthau should play the judge. He even looks a little like him, don't you think?"

I was flabbergasted. I didn't say a word. But from that day on, I *knew*. I *never* had a chance with Lorraine Abraham. A few minutes later she stood up and held out her arms to take away my sleeping baby. "It's time," was all she said.

# Chapter 12

# Delays

Judge Sorkow surely knew that the temporary custody order almost always becomes the permanent order. He structured his task to justify his original May 5 order.

—George Annas in "At Law,"
a publication of the Hastings Center,
June 1987

**O**n October 17, 1986, the law firm of Cassidy, Foss, Despo & San Filippo agreed to represent me. The overwhelming amount of time and resources demanded by the case made it impossible for Alan Grosman, Bob Arenstein, or any other single attorney to continue the work alone. Nevertheless, both Grosman and Arenstein remained supportive and involved throughout the entire case. Harold Cassidy's firm had decided to represent me without a retainer, and to forgive any fees that I could not afford to pay.

For that contact I had Alison Ward to thank. As a young unwed mother, Alison gave up a baby for adoption, then was reunited with her after fourteen years. She had followed my story in the press and called to suggest that I meet with Harold Cassidy's law firm. Cassidy, she explained, had experience working with biological mothers who had given up their babies for adoption and then changed their minds. Alison arranged a meeting, and I was delighted when the soft-spoken, forty-one-year-old attorney from Red Bank, New Jersey, agreed to head my defense team. In the months that followed, Alison Ward kept files of the litigation, screened the media, brought gifts for Sara, and provided an ongoing source of support and friendship.

The trial was scheduled to begin on November 3, but Bill and Betsy Stern and Gary Skoloff knew that in child-custody cases, possession is nine-tenths of the law. The longer Sara remained with the Sterns, the greater was the chance that she would stay there forever. Every delay in the start of the trial would work against us. Every single day that passed would make it less likely that any court, including the New Jersey Supreme Court, would ever change the baby's custody for *any* reason short of abuse or neglect.

So no one was surprised when Gary Skoloff argued that he needed at least two more months to prepare for the trial. The Appellate Division of the New Jersey Superior Court turned down his request, saying, "It is in the best interests of the child that the trial commence on November third."

Skoloff's request was followed by two short delays that Harold Cassidy agreed to. The first was a ten-day delay that Judge Sorkow said was necessary in order to give the attorneys more time to prepare. However, he simultaneously denied Harold's request to have legal experts argue that the contract I had signed was illegal.

"I'm not going to be mired in inquiries dealing with

ethics, morality, and theology," the judge said. "That's not the court's function."

The second delay was announced by Sorkow on November 7. This time the date was changed to November 17 so that the judge could consider a petition by three New Jersey newspapers, the *Asbury Park Press*, the Newark *Star-Ledger*, and the *Bergen Record*, to make the results of Elizabeth Stern's fertility tests public. But after this delay, Judge Sorkow flatly denied the request. Not only had he decided to keep the results of the fertility tests secret from the media, saying "Betsy Stern's right to privacy outweighed the right of the public to view the entire case," he had also decided that the results should be kept secret from me. He announced that although I was a litigant, I would be barred from the courtroom when Betsy's fertility or medical condition was being discussed.

When lawyers for the newspapers appealed the decision, Harold Cassidy also appealed. On November 21, the New Jersey Supreme Court and the Appellate Division reversed Sorkow's decision. The Supreme Court ruled that I should be permitted to attend all courtroom discussions, and the Appellate Division ruled that the matter should be made public.

But, back on November 14, Skoloff had asked for an additional delay of two *months*. Saying that the mounting pretrial appeals forced him to put the trial off, Sorkow granted Skoloff's request. Over my attorney's objections, he announced that the new trial date would be January 5.

Then, just four days later, on November 18, Sorkow ordered a delay of a different kind. This time he said that, unless he divided the upcoming trial into two separate trials, dealing first with the legality of the surrogate contract and then, at a later date, with the custody issue, all of the pretrial preparations could not be completed by January 5.

"I'm prepared to try this case on Monday," said Harold Cassidy. "I'm against any further adjournment or the dividing of the trial. Justice delayed is justice denied," he told the press. Once again he returned to the Appellate Division and appealed the judge's ruling. On December 3, the Appellate Division reversed Judge Sorkow and directed that there be only one trial, on all the issues.

Gary Skoloff complained about this decision, saying that it changed "the entire game plan" of the case, making it difficult for him to prepare in time for the January 5 trial. He appealed the ruling to the New Jersey Supreme Court.

Lorraine Abraham not only supported Skoloff's position, but threatened to resign if she could not get the necessary psychological, psychiatric, and social-work studies on the parents completed by January 5.

Apparently unmoved by Abraham's threat, the Supreme Court affirmed the Appellate Division's decision and again ordered one trial.

The day before Christmas, Sorkow announced that we would have a two-week hiatus between the contract and custody phases of the trial. This was not an outright violation of the Appellate Division and Supreme Court orders, but it was clearly a violation of the spirit of the order, and, of course, it was prejudicial to me. In effect, we ended up with two trials.

At that point I was so discouraged by all the delays and so broke that I decided we wouldn't celebrate Christmas. Luckily, Harold Cassidy wouldn't allow it. He called the kids and told them to make a Christmas list, then arrived laden with gifts. It was the first of many times that Harold Cassidy went far beyond his legal commitment and befriended our entire family.

# Chapter 13

# The Trial Begins

No one who visits the "Baby M" trial at the Bergen County Courthouse in Hackensack could hope to view its processes with an eye as experienced as Richard Whitehead's. He is a sanitation truck driver and the Baby M case is an exercise in compacting and disposing of trash. The package designated as trash is his wife, Mary Beth Whitehead, mother and inconvenience.

—Murray Kempton in *Newsday*,
February 27, 1987

**A**fter five months of motions, appeals, and delays, on January 5, 1987, in the heart of a cold, snowy winter, the trial finally began. The second-floor courtoom was small and proper, with blue and white trim and walls that had been painted to depict Revolutionary scenes. As steam hissed from the old radiators, sketch artists crammed into the jury box and scratched in ink and felt-tipped pens. Thirty-eight of the fifty-four seats in the courtroom were reserved for reporters, who had stood in line since 6:00 A.M.

Every major newspaper from New York to California, as well as England's *Manchester Guardian* and France's *Paris-Match*, was there. The local TV and radio stations and the national networks also attended, reporting our struggle to millions of Americans. Skoloff began the proceedings by attempting to weave a case based more on sympathy for the Sterns than on medical fact or legal substance. "The issue to be decided in this court," he said, addressing the press directly, "is whether a promise to make the gift of life should be enforced. . . . Mary Beth Whitehead agreed to give Bill Stern a child of his own flesh and blood, which Bill and Betsy Stern most desperately wanted but could not risk because fate had stricken Betsy with one of the most serious diseases known to man, multiple sclerosis." Skoloff paused, waiting for his words to sink in. "The medical condition rendered her, as a practical matter, infertile," he continued, "and the Sterns were forced to realize that because of Elizabeth Stern's medical condition, she could not carry a baby without significant risk to her health."

When Skoloff had finished his explanation, Judge Harvey Sorkow slowly raised his head, revealing heavy jowls and a slightly hooked, bulbous nose. He seemed satisfied with the explanation.

But Harold Cassidy was not satisfied. He looked at Judge Sorkow intently, studying his face. He had noticed that Sorkow seemed very much inclined toward Gary Skoloff's argument. "There is no real reason why Betsy Stern could not have conceived," he said when it was his turn to speak. "The only reason that the Sterns did not attempt to conceive a child was . . . because Mrs. Stern had a career that had to be advanced. . . . What you're going to find is that multiple sclerosis, as horrible as it sounds, comes in three types, and what Mrs. Stern has is diagnosed as the mildest form. She was never even diagnosed until after we deposed her in this case. That's how bad it was. You're going to find that it's almost as though it's an afterthought. . . . The record is also going to indicate that no attempts were ever made to conceive a child. . . . We're here," he continued, "not because Betsy Stern is infertile but because one woman stood up and said there are some things that money can't buy."

Bill Stern shook his head again and again in negation, and when he finally took the stand, as Gary Skoloff's first witness, he was very pale. With beads of sweat on his upper lip, he recalled his childhood.

He was born in Berlin in 1946, where his parents had hidden from the Nazis for five years. When he was two, they traveled to the United States and settled in a lower-middle-class section of Pittsburgh. His father worked the night shift as a short-order cook in a bar and grill, and his mother worked in a factory, putting rubber stripping on storm windows. He was, by his own account, the center of their world—an only child who "never had to share." When he was twelve, his father died. Bill and his mother later moved to New York, where Bill got a bachelor's degree from New York University before going to graduate school at the University of Michigan. There, while working on a Ph.D. in biochemistry, he met Betsy.

Bill and Betsy were in a class together in 1967, but didn't get to know each other until two years later, at a party. Despite his Jewish background, Bill Stern and Betsy, who is Methodist, were married by a minister in a church wedding. They had, he explained, decided to postpone having children until Betsy completed her residency.

Then, in minute detail, Bill described how they had first learned that Betsy might have MS. She woke up one morning in 1979 with blurred vision, and she wept when an ophthalmologist told her that she suffered from optic neuritis, an inflammation of the optic nerve and a possible sign of MS. But, he acknowledged, with a note of hesitancy in his voice, Betsy recovered from the vision problem and never went to a neurologist to find if she actually *had* MS.

Over a fifteen-year period she had occasionally experienced weakness and slight numbness in her leg, fingers, and toes during hot and muggy weather. Those, along with the single incident of optic neuritis, were her only symptoms.

At that point in the testimony, it was becoming painfully apparent that even my original longing to help an infertile couple had been thwarted. The next day an in-depth survey of medical experts conducted by the *Bergen Record* made my understanding even clearer. Now I knew why the Sterns had fought so hard to keep Betsy's condition from me and from the public. As far as anyone could tell, she was no more infertile than I was, and according to the experts contacted by the press, there was no medical reason for her not to become pregnant and have her own baby.

Dr. Lawrence W. Myers, professor of neurology and director of a multiple sclerosis research clinic at UCLA, said, when interviewed by the press, "MS is *not* a reason to avoid pregnancy." He then added, "Lots of women with MS have normal, healthy pregnancies without a bad effect on their MS, or their health in general."

"It's no longer a debated issue," said Dr. Randall T. Schapiro, a neurology professor at the University of Minnesota and director of the Fairview Multiple Sclerosis Center in Minneapolis. "People with MS can get pregnant and deliver healthy babies just as naturally as women who do not have MS."

Dr. David Thomas, a Connecticut neurologist who had led a recent study at the Rocky Mountain Multiple Sclerosis Center, concluded the newspaper interview. He said, "Having a child makes no difference in the course of MS."

After that revelation, Bill and Betsy and I seemed to grow farther and farther apart. Separated from each other by a bank of attorneys and a lawyers' table cluttered with legal pads, briefcases, and official-looking documents, Bill and Betsy no longer even looked at me. They also avoided walking out of the courtroom at the same time that I did.

Yet, despite my anger, I often thought about how sad it was that we had come to this point. And that all of us were in so much pain. Sometimes I felt as if the whole horrible struggle was crushing my spirit.

Reporters who had been following the case for months told me that I looked weary and tense. They asked me what had happened to the funny, high-spirited, combative Mary Beth that they had grown so used to.

"Hey," I said weakly, "we're going to win."

Only Gary Skoloff looked confident. He continued to crack jokes as he paced before the judge, and insisted that the entire case was no more than a simple contract dispute. "Four intelligent adults came together," he liked to say. "They made an agreement. Two didn't carry it out, and that is why we are here today."

Harold Cassidy still maintained that the contract was both immoral and illegal and that it violated all of the laws that had been so carefully drafted by the state legislature to protect the interests of helpless babies.

But as I watched Harold through those long days, I could see a subtle change taking place in him, much like the change that reporters had observed in me. During the preliminary hearings he had strode jauntily around the courtroom, looking poised and enthusiastic. By the middle of the second week of the trial, it had become painfully

obvious that anyone who represented me would be dis-
liked by Judge Sorkow. The judge had made his displeas-
ure clear from the beginning by coldly denying almost
every objection Cassidy made. He constantly interrupted
him, cut him off at every juncture, and actually told him
to "sit down and be silent." Harold Cassidy was clearly in
the unenviable position of confronting a hostile judge
from the very beginning of the trial.

While Cassidy had hoped to give the judge a deeper
level of insight into my character, he was stopped before
he could begin. After Bill and Betsy had testified, Harold
asked me to describe my pregnancy and the day of Sara's
birth. He was cut off immediately. Sorkow had listened
patiently to all of Betsy Stern's medical testimony and had
even allowed the Sterns to describe, in minute detail, how
they selected wallpaper for the baby's room.

"Originally," Betsy said, ". . . we got these teddy
bear stencils . . . that was one of the cutest patterns. We
picked out some wallpaper . . . and it didn't match."

"Her room had this ugly old paper," Bill added. "I
rented a steamer. . . . I was ankle-deep in pieces of paper.
We found . . . a teddy bear print . . . and this little border
to go with it."

Now, however, Sorkow refused to listen. "We don't
have to go through the pain of birth," he told Cassidy.
"The child was born. The child was born."

By the second week, Judge Sorkow had become so
testy in his responses that members of the press expressed
surprise when he cracked a smile. Sorkow's anger only
seemed to increase when Harold introduced, as his last
witness in the contract phase of the trial, Dr. Gerard
Lehrer, a neurologist who teaches at Mount Sinai School
of Medicine.

Lehrer took the stand and explained that Betsy had

"a very, very, very slight case of MS, if any. . . . If she were a rational physician, she would have taken steps to confirm the diagnosis. There's an old adage that a doctor who treats himself has a fool for a patient and a greater fool for a doctor." The judge glared at Dr. Lehrer as Harold Cassidy concluded the presentation of the first part of his case.

When the second stage of the trial finally began after the two-week hiatus, the first thing the press noticed was that I was being represented by Harold Cassidy's associate, Randy Wolf. Harold, who now expected defeat, had stayed in the office to begin work on the Supreme Court appeals. The press was still wondering if Cassidy had withdrawn because of a personality conflict with the judge, when they noticed that Gary Skoloff's style had changed. His easy, joking manner had become decidedly more cynical.

"As to Mary Beth," Skoloff said during the opening session of the custody phase of the trial, frowning as if even my name left a bad taste in his mouth, "we're going to produce thirty-five factors that I wish to enumerate to Your Honor right now. Thirty-five factors weighing against custody of the baby to Mary Beth Whitehead."

First, Skoloff claimed that I had intentionally and flagrantly disobeyed an order of the court by going to Florida with Sara. From there he went on to cite everything, from Tuesday changing schools and Rick losing his job, to my baby-sitting for my niece without pay, as reasons to deprive me of custody and justify my termination. "If there is one case in the United States," Skoloff concluded contemptuously, "where joint custody will not work, where visitation rights will not work, where maintaining parental rights will not work, this is it. Your Honor, under both the contract theory and the best-interest theory, you *must* terminate the rights of Mary Beth Whitehead and allow Betsy Stern to adopt. It is the only way Betsy Stern will be Melissa's mother. Otherwise, it is not what everyone agreed to and understood. Otherwise, Betsy Stern will not be the mother of Melissa. . . . Judge, I know you are extremely interested in protecting the baby, and the baby's only chance is to grant custody to William Stern. Terminate the parental rights of Mary Beth Whitehead and allow Bill Stern and Betsy Stern to be Melissa's mother and father."

Lorraine Abraham had also decided to announce in court that she too wanted Sara's custody to go *exclusively* to the Sterns, but, unlike Gary Skoloff, she tried to appear neutral. She paced herself carefully, presenting herself as an impartial advocate of the baby's best interests.

"What are the best—not the *better* but the *best—* interests of this child?" she asked rhetorically, then paused and smiled at the judge. "To me she is no longer Baby M, she is Melissa Elizabeth Stern, or Sara Elizabeth Whitehead. She is a human being now ten months old. This inquiry as to her best interests consists of presenting facts and expert opinions to this court. . . . In that sense, this trial is like any other custody trial, despite the worldwide attention that has been focused on it. What this trial also has in common with all custody trials is the pain and the anguish of the adults involved. Fortunately, the child is too young yet to perceive the extraordinary human emotions that will be displayed here." Then, motioning toward me with her right hand, she added, "No human being with a modicum of sensitivity can fail to empathize and sympathize with all concerned."

After that, Lorraine Abraham winced. She pressed her fingers to her temples and massaged them as if what she was about to say caused her to experience actual physical pain. "I knew that the day would come," she continued, "when I would have to stand before this court and present a recommendation, when I would have to bring this court all that I perceive to be an exposition of the child's best interests. The test of making a recommendation has weighed heavily on me during these past six months as I have come to know and understand all of the parties. It has caused many a sleepless night and has compelled me to look beyond myself for the answers."

Abraham paused again. She shuffled some papers. Then she added, "I chose three individuals. I felt one was not enough and I chose them from three different disciplines: Doctor Judith Brown Greif, a doctor of social work with experience in family therapy; Doctor David Brodzinsky, a clinical and developmental psychologist; and Doctor Marshall Schechter, an extremely respected psychiatrist. As each individual is offered to the court, I believe it will be impressed by the wealth of experience each brings to this investigation. I believe," she added, glancing toward the judge, "that the court will come to appreciate the independence and dedication each has brought to his or her task. The plan for their task was designed by each of them. It was to interview the adults individually and . . . to observe each of the family units with the baby in their most ideal circumstances, their respective homes. . . . My only request," she added, pausing for emphasis, "was that each of these individuals reach their own *independent* conclusions."

What Lorraine Abraham did not explain, as she stood before the court stressing the importance of "independent conclusions," was why, on December 13, 1986, prior to any of the interviews, as Marshall Schechter revealed in his report, the three experts met with each other and with her, and discussed the case for approximately eight hours. Nor did she mention that their meeting continued the next day and that they met a third time to compare notes at the conclusion of their observations. She also neglected to say that those three experts conducted most of their interviews and observations together.

Finally, Lorraine Abraham failed to remind the court that Sara was brought into my house in December for just four hours, after not having been there since May 5, when she was only five weeks old. Nor did she point out that Sara had not been permitted to see Rick or Ryan or Tuesday for six months, and that her contacts with me had been restricted to the two-hour guarded visits at the Conklin Center twice a week.

"I ask the court to bear in mind their independence," she repeated once again, "and their expertise coming from three different disciplines and three orientations. And yet," she added, shaking her head in bewilderment, as if we were about to witness some kind of astonishing coincidence or design of fate, "they will each recommend to this court that custody be awarded to the Sterns and visitation be denied at this time." Lorraine Abraham added, "I am compelled by the overwhelming weight of their investigation to join in their recommendation."

# Chapter 14

# The Assault Against My Character

Day after day they hacked away at her. They called forth a stream of so-called expert witnesses. . . . The witnesses assailed Mrs. Whitehead's character, her intelligence, her mental balance, her past, her present, her husband and her finances. . . . One day the Sterns may regret the pain that they have caused Baby M's natural mother.

—Joice Booth in *This Week*,
Portland, Oregon, March 14, 1987

**T**wo days later Betsy Stern took the stand. "My typical weekday with Melissa," she said, cocking her head to one side, "starts at about eight o'clock, when Bill and Melissa come into the bedroom. Bill gives me a peck on the cheek. He leans Melissa over the bed so she can give me a little kiss on the cheek, too. And I'm up right away, because he plops her down on the bed and she is poking her hands in my eyes and my mouth and pulling my hair, and she's all over the place."

Suddenly an image of Bill and Betsy creating a family with my baby flashed before me. I imagined Sara being trained to kiss Betsy Stern each morning. An overwhelming sense of despair gripped me as I thought about not being able to hear her say "Mama" for the first time, or to see her take her first steps. I was glad when my thoughts were interrupted by Gary Skoloff's next question.

"What activities do you personally enjoy, that you're looking forward to doing with Melissa as she gets older?" he asked.

"Well," Betsy responded, "I'm really looking forward to taking her to *The Nutcracker Suite* every year. I'd like to sort of make that a family tradition. I was an aspiring ballet dancer," she added with a smile, "but my mother made me quit because I wasn't practicing much."

"Did you take lessons?"

"I did. Second grade through fourth grade. So I'm really looking forward to taking her to see that. Bill and I have gone to see it a couple of times, but I always looked at the kids. They really enjoy that."

"Betsy," said Skoloff, "if Bill gets custody, what is your position with reference to the Whiteheads having contact with Melissa now?"

Betsy's face hardened, her manner changed. She leaned forward in her seat and narrowed her eyes. "I wouldn't want it," she said, clenching her fists. "I don't think it would ever work, and I think it would be very detrimental to Melissa. It could destroy her."

"Could you state your reasons?"

"Well," Betsy repeated, "I think that it would be very detrimental." She paused as if lost for words.

"Go on, go on," Skoloff urged. "It's all right."

"I think it would be very detrimental for Melissa," Betsy said for a third time.

"Why?" Gary Skoloff pressed.

"Because," Betsy answered, with her face growing red and her eyes flashing, "I am extremely angry at Mary

Beth for making this case unsealed. . . . For that I can't ever forgive her." Betsy Stern was apparently referring to the fact that the case had become a matter of public record. "I have absolutely no trust in her whatever anymore. I don't know how we could ever come to any agreement," Betsy continued. "I don't know how to mend fences with somebody that manipulates me, that lies to me whenever she tells me anything. She doesn't seem to respect our parenthood. She still refers to my husband as Mr. Sperm Donor. I think she would undermine my abilities to be a mother."

"Mrs. Stern," Harold Cassidy's associate, Randy Wolf, said during his cross-examination, "it's true that you told Mary Beth Whitehead all along during the pregnancy that she could have visitation with the child, isn't it?"

"Not all along," Betsy answered. "But somewhere around a couple of months, four or five months after she became pregnant, Mary Beth asked me if Ryan could come see the baby. She had asked on another occasion if she could come visit, and I did say yes."

Then, homing in on another important issue, Wolf said, "Do you remember having a conversation with Mary Beth Whitehead on April twelfth at her home?"

"Yes," Betsy said, frowning.

"And do you remember saying, 'I don't want this to go to court. It's messy and expensive. Your lawyers are going to dig up mud about us and our lawyers are going to dig up mud about you and throw it at you'?"

"Yes," Betsy acknowledged reluctantly.

"Did you tell her that?" Wolf repeated, pushing his advantage.

"Yes," she answered. Only this time her voice was

barely audible. Wolf paused to let Betsy's admission sink in.

"And did you," he said when he resumed the questioning, "believe at that time that slinging mud was an appropriate way to handle who should keep the baby?"

"Object, Your Honor," Skoloff shouted, jumping to his feet. "Argumentative."

"Mr. Wolf," the judge said after having the statement reread to him, "I will sustain the objection."

Nevertheless, Randy Wolf had made his point. "Is it true," he asked, returning to the earlier line of questioning, "that if you had your own wishes about it, you would not permit Ryan or Tuesday to visit Melissa—or Baby M, as we refer to her—until she's fourteen to eighteen years old?"

"Yes, if I had my own wishes I would," Betsy answered.

"And it's true also that if your own wishes were followed, Mary Beth would not be permitted to visit the child until the child was already a teenager?"

"Yes," Betsy said, "for the reasons I gave earlier. I do not think any ongoing or periodic visits would be good for her."

"Were you concerned about what effect taking the baby away from Mary Beth Whitehead would have on the baby?"

"I knew it would be hard on Mary Beth," Betsy said, "and in Melissa's best interest."

Wolf then asked her about the baby's health when she was seized from me in Florida. "Did the baby appear to be in good physical condition?"

"Yes," Betsy admitted.

"Did she appear to be happy?"

"Yes," Betsy said hesitantly.

"Now, I believe you testified that if Mary Beth White-head receives custody of the baby, you don't want to visit."

"That is correct," Betsy said. "I do not want to visit."

"Now, if you are awarded custody, you do not want Mary Beth Whitehead to have visitation," Wolf said. "Is that correct?"

"Yes," Betsy answered quietly.

"What are your feelings," Wolf asked, pressing her, "about contact with her birth mother?"

Betsy shifted in her seat, then said, "Would you define 'contact' for me?"

Wolf nodded. "Meeting her in person. First on a very occasional basis, once a year, say."

"I would not like that," Betsy answered, her face flushing. "If you mean by 'contact' that she meets her once to satisfy her curiosity, fine. I know that children who are adopted, some of them, want to meet their biological mothers. And when she is whatever the age, twelve or fourteen or sixteen, if she wants to know Mary Beth's name, I would tell her. . . . But as I said, I think any ongoing or periodic contact would be detrimental."

As soon as Betsy had left the witness stand and before I could testify, Gary Skoloff played the tapes of the telephone conversations that Bill Stern had secretly recorded while I was in Florida.

Then, during the recess, he handed out copies of the tapes and printed transcripts of the conversations to the media. That night every major network played the most damaging statements out of context. Although Skoloff had been describing the tapes for months, hearing them in court and on the evening news—the day before I was scheduled to take the stand—left me so badly shaken that it was difficult for me to testify.

\* \* \*

The next morning, when the press accounts appeared, I refused to look at them. I knew that it would take all my courage just to get on the stand. With trembling hands I glanced at Judge Sorkow. He glared back. I looked away, frightened by the coldness of his eyes.

"How do you feel about your children?" Randy Wolf asked.

"They're my life," I answered, vaguely surprised to hear that my voice was barely above a whisper. "I don't have any skills to really speak of, but the skill I know I do well is being a mother, and no one can take that away from me. No one," I repeated, gaining strength from the depth of my conviction. "It's one of the things I do best, and I'm not ashamed to say it. I know that I'd be an excellent mother for Sara."

"What kind of activities do you engage in with your children?" Randy asked. "What do you do together?"

"Well," I answered, "we go to mass together. I take them back and forth to catechism classes and to soccer. I keep them sparkling clean and immaculate all the time. That's my job, and you know whatever it is I'll do it, whatever it takes. When they're sick, I'm the one who goes in to them. I'm the one who's there for them when they need to talk. I dance with them, sing with them. They love to sing together. I wouldn't publicly sing with them. But in the privacy of our house we sing. They like me to play the piano with them. I teach them two wrongs don't make a right. Every night they sit at the kitchen table together and do their homework. If they have trouble, I help. . . . There is no limit to anything I would do for my children. Whatever it might be."

"Mary Beth," Randy said gently, "if you don't get custody of Sara, do you want to see her?"

"Yes," I answered emphatically. "I'm her mother, and

whether this court only lets me see her two minutes a week, two hours a week, or two days, I'm her mother and I want to see her, no matter what."

As the morning progressed, I regained my composure. But during the noon recess, I learned that at the very same time I was testifying, the court clerk was handing out copies of the reports that Lorraine Abraham's hired experts had compiled. The impact was a double blow. Not only had the court and the reporters not heard me enough to report on what I said, but I had been further discredited by the negative documents the press had been given. The next day the *Washington Post* wrote, "As Mary Beth Whitehead appealed today to keep the baby she bore for a childless couple, a report was released in which mental health experts called her immature, narcissistic, impulsive and histrionic. . . . Marshall D. Schechter, a University of Pennsylvania Medical School professor, wrote, 'She has a mixed personality disorder which does not yield readily to any form of treatment.' "

"Even as she was presenting her case," the Newark *Star-Ledger* added, "the court yesterday released a set of reports by three experts hired by Abraham that could severely damage her cause. All say that Stern should get custody of the baby and that Whitehead should be barred from seeing her until the child is at least five years old."

As soon as I was off the witness stand, Skoloff's team launched still another attack. They called Lee Salk to the stand. Salk was a psychologist whose personal life had become controversial in 1975, when New York Judge Guy Ribaudo awarded him sole custody of his son and daughter. The judge had used an "affirmative standard" to decide which parent was "better fit to guide the development of the children and their future," and had chosen the parent with more money and education. Salk, who had never met or interviewed me, had based his own recommendation exclusively on the findings of Abraham's experts.

"Doctor," began Gary Skoloff's poker-faced co-counsel, Frank Donahue, "you were retained by the Sterns in this matter."

"Yes, I was," Salk said. "I was retained for the purposes of determining what would be in the best interest of Baby M. Mrs. Stern," he continued, "is far and away much more capable of meeting the needs of Baby M, and providing a kind of care that would be in her best interest. . . ."

Then, reading from his notes, Salk quoted Abraham's experts and called me immature, exhibitionistic, and histrionic. He said he agreed with Marshall Schechter's appraisal of a mixed personality disorder.

"You've concluded," Donahue continued without expression, "that Mrs. Whitehead's contact with the child should be terminated. And you've mentioned that in your testimony. Can you tell me why?"

"Well, yes," Salk said, looking up from his report for the first time. "But the legal term that's been used is 'termination of parental rights,' and I don't see that there were any 'parental rights' that existed in the first place. As I see it," he continued matter-of-factly, "Mr. Stern and Mrs. Whitehead entered into an agreement that was clearly understood by both. The agreement involved the provision of an ovum by Mrs. Whitehead for artificial insemination in exchange for ten thousand dollars . . . and so my feeling is that in both structural and functional terms, Mr. and Mrs. Stern's role as parents was achieved by a surrogate uterus and not a surrogate mother."

\* \* \*

"I don't want to overreact to the 'surrogate uterus' comment," Cassidy, who had returned to court as an observer that day, said calmly when court adjourned, "but I was repulsed by it. It's inhumane. There's no other word for it. It doesn't take into consideration what a woman really is."

Other people apparently agreed. For the first time the attempt to discredit me seemed to have gone one step too far. Slowly, almost imperceptibly, public opinion began to shift. It started when journalists, who still supported the Sterns and wanted the baby to remain with them, began wondering out loud in print about the ethics and the tactics that were being used against me.

"The Sterns have more money, more education and a more stable home life," wrote the *Camden County Courier Post*. "Baby M . . . should go to the Sterns and yet . . . Salk said some chilling things that say a lot about where our society will end up if surrogate contracts are legitimatized. Is not the bond between mother and child the most fundamental among human beings? If you devalue that bond, casually dismiss it as simply the lending of a uterus, what does that imply about how much we truly value all our relationships to each other and human life itself?"

Ellen Goodman of the *Boston Globe* added her voice to that of the *Courier Post*. She too sided with the Sterns. "As a custody judge," she said, "I would award the baby to the Sterns." Nevertheless, she acknowledged that there was something about the inequity of this case that was eating away at her:

In the Baby M trial, *M* stands for money. . . . Nobody suggests in court that the wife of a garbage man and the husband of a pediatrician are not equal under the law. . . . But it is money . . . that may well decide her custody. . . .

> Three experts say Baby's M's mother is unstable. . . .
> Those "experts" are more confident than this reader in
> judging Mary Beth's behavior. What if this mother was
> driven to "craziness" by the loss of the child and then lost
> it because she sounded crazy?
>
> We are talking about money. Mary Beth worked
> briefly as a go-go dancer . . . [but] what should a high
> school dropout, who married at sixteen, and had her first
> child at seventeen, do for a living when she's separated
> from her husband? Brain surgery? Add another twenty
> thousand dollars a year to the Whitehead bank account
> and would the family suddenly become more stable? Stable
> enough? A stronger contender for Baby M?

But it wasn't just newspaper columnists who had begun
to wonder what this trial was *really* about. Unknown to
me, for several weeks a number of well-known feminists
had been arguing about taking a public stand. Many
disapproved of the fact that I had dropped out of high
school and married so young. They felt that I glorified the
role of a pregnant, economically dependent housewife.
Some also believed that a woman should have the right to
do whatever she wanted with her body, including selling
it. Others felt that surrogacy represented a solution for
career women who didn't want to be troubled with childbearing. Several of the women argued that the main difference between me and millions of other women engaged
in custody battles was simply that I had signed a surrogacy contract rather than a marriage contract. Whatever
their differences, all of the feminists had been appalled by
Lee Salk's comment, and they now agreed that my public
degradation and loss was a threat to all women.

On February 18, eight of these women, including a
psychologist, a professor, and a psychiatrist, decided to

speak out. Calling themselves the Committee for Mothers' Rights, the group appeared at the courthouse and held a press conference.

Dr. Phyllis Chesler, New York author, psychologist, and associate professor, stood at a microphone inside the press room and spoke to reporters:

> We are here today to support Mary Beth Whitehead's custody claim. We are here today to denounce this trial as a form of child abuse and sex discrimination. We are here today to demand the return of Baby Sara to her loving mother, Mary Beth Whitehead. We are here today to remind everyone that Mary Beth Whitehead has made a mistake and in her way is trying to set it right. It is barbaric to punish her so heavily for having made a mistake. Who will cast the first stone? Mary is not a murderer, she has not abused or abandoned her children. She is our Mary, the mother of a child who happens to have no genetic relationship to her legal husband. . . . She refused money. She established a maternal bond with her daughter and continued to love and want her child in the face of enormous obstacles.
>
> We recognize that William Stern has an investment in parenting a genetically related child. We understand that he and his wife, Elizabeth, have developed parental feelings for Sara Whitehead. But we ask, what kind of people would use money, power, legal tactics and legal claims to so violently grab an infant from her mother's arms without regard for the effect it would have on mother and child? We wonder what kind of people would bring legal proceedings against a child's natural mother which are intended to slander and malign her character. And which cause enormous suffering to her and her family. Do the Sterns truly believe thay can raise Sara without ever having her find out about her natural mother, the tremendous love her mother bears for her or the ugly record of this case?

After Dr. Chesler spoke, the committee handed out statements to the press that explained that as feminists and as women and mothers, they had been asked again and again "not to take sides." Essentially not to take my side. They called the case a terrifying but not a unique miscarriage of justice, a brutal use of state power against one family. They concluded that while everyone, including women and mothers, had been blaming me, I was actually the victim in this case.

I knew that these women saw me as a symbol for something far larger than my case. Several of the women openly expressed a fear that society's acceptance of the practice of surrogacy would lead to an increasing number of women being viewed as uteruses for hire. And ultimately, when one woman's egg could be implanted easily in another woman's womb, it could lead to "baby farms," where Third World women could bear babies for wealthy American couples. They were deeply concerned about the dangers of exploitation in a marketplace based on women's economic poverty, male genetic narcissism, and the greed of middlemen, like Noel Keane, who grew rich from surrogate arrangements.

As the women rallied outside to support me, inside the courtroom Dr. Donald Klein, a psychiatrist and professor at Columbia University College of Physicians and Surgeons, took the stand on my behalf. Dr. Klein was one of the authors of the textbook on mental disorders that Lorraine Abraham's experts had quoted from. He said that I did not have any serious personality problems, was not mentally disabled, and did not need therapy. Klein, who strongly disagreed with Marshall Schechter, pointed out that all of the examples Schechter had used in his report to support his accusations were taken from the past year. "This is a very sharp disruption in her life," he explained. "It is not a pattern. It's a derailment."

During a recess outside the courtroom, when Klein was asked about the telephone conversations that Bill Stern had recorded, he said to reporters, "She was desperate; she was trying to get Mr. Stern to back off. You use any stick to beat a dog. That's what it comes down to."

Even though Schechter had not yet taken the stand, Klein analyzed the widely publicized evidence that Schechter had used to diagnose me and systematically discredited it. Klein said that all three court-appointed experts had violated the diagnostic standards defined by the textbook and endorsed by the American Psychiatric Association. Those standards assert that the psychiatric traits for personality disorders must be exhibited on a "chronic" and "enduring" long-term basis, from adolescence to adulthood. He said that "Schechter's evaluation was made in the context of 'the current ruckus' and 'ignored' the most important issues. A diagnosis of personality disorder cannot be based on actions a person has taken during a specific period of 'tremendous conflict,' but must depend on 'repeated showing of the traits throughout life.' "

Klein had the same criticism for the more moderate assessments of Brodzinsky and Greif, who had tagged me as "impulsive, egocentric, self-dramatic, manipulative and exploitative." He said that the standard for diagnosing personality disorders was rewritten a few years ago, precisely to avoid this kind of mistaken diagnosis. The text he had coauthored clearly stated that the traits be viewed over the long term, but, he added, Schechter and the others had not made the "slightest attempt" to show that the traits they described were enduring.

Despite Dr. Klein's rebuttal, and the increasing public support that I was receiving, Lorraine Abraham's experts had done a huge amount of damage. More than two weeks before any of them had even taken the stand, the reports had not only been handed out to the press, but had been printed in every major newspaper. The assessments had permeated the entire second half of the trial.

By the time Marshall Schechter finally took the stand, on February 23, everyone in the courtroom thought they knew exactly what he was going to say. As it turned out, he actually said a lot of things we weren't expecting to hear. He told Lorraine Abraham that the reason the experts observed the baby in our respective homes was that "children build up anxiety going into strange circumstances." Of course, Sara hadn't been in my house since she was five weeks old, and by that standard it did indeed represent a strange place.

To my amazement, Schechter also told the court that he and the other experts wanted to observe how well she knew us and how attached she was. Of course, since Sara had only been allowed to see Ryan, Tuesday, and Rick once since she was taken from us in Florida, they were actually strangers to her. Even I had seen her only during those two-hour visits supervised by guards. Nevertheless, Schechter said, "We were there to see if there were some specific attachment behaviors and feelings of loss when, for example, any one of the Whitehead family left the room.

"I took a chair out of the kitchen," Schechter continued, "and sat by the fireplace and just literally, throughout the entire four to five hours' time, observed the baby. Their interaction, the reaction of Ryan and Tuesday to the child and to the parents." At that point, one of my attorneys wanted to stand up and point out that we had no fireplace, but he held his tongue. "The Whiteheads' living room is well furnished," Schechter said. "I think better than the Sterns', if I can make a judgment on that." He added that the baby responded "beautifully" to all of us and that she began to whimper and attempted to crawl after me when I left the room. After that he launched his attack.

My first mistake was in saying "hooray." "Initially, on our coming in, when Mrs. Whitehead said something to her like 'play patty-cake,' the baby didn't do anything. When the baby did get picked up and sat on Mrs. Whitehead's lap, she clapped her hands. Mrs. Whitehead's response was 'Hooray.' That is, she was saying 'hooray' instead of 'patty-cake.' "

My next mistake was providing the wrong play equipment. "The toys," Schechter explained, "were essentially four different pandas, all stuffed animals in varying sizes from essentially one foot to about four or five feet in height. Plus a bear that had inserted in it a tape recorder that responded immediately when someone spoke into the tape and repeated exactly the same thing. And now, recognizing that they did not have the baby all of the time, I certainly would wonder about their putting their best foot forward and giving the baby the kind of toys nine-month-old babies play best with. Namely pots and pans or spoons, as something which is much more characteristic of the needs of the baby, rather than these enormous panda dolls."

"On the basis of your clinical observations," Lorraine Abraham asked Schechter later that afternoon, "were you able to form an opinion as to whether any of the adults you interviewed in this matter had a diagnosable mental disorder?"

"Yes, I did."

"And which individual was that?" she continued, as if everyone in the courtroom didn't already know.

His eyes traveled the room. "That was Mary Beth Whitehead," he said accusingly. "And the diagnosis that I arrived at was mixed personality disorder."

Marshall Schechter took a moment to explain to the court that a diagnosis of a mixed personality disorder is used when a person does not meet the criteria of any *specific* disorder, but displays features from several categories of personality disorders. Then Dr. Schechter told the court that one category, "borderline personality disorder," was displayed when I resisted giving my nursing infant to the police of May 5.

"Certainly," he explained, "one of the big elements is handing the baby out of the window to Mr. Whitehead as an unpredictable, impulsive act that falls under this category."

"And under 'narcissistic personality disorder,' what traits did you consider?" Lorraine Abraham inquired.

"Her sense of entitlement. Her consideration that, just because she's the mother, she knows what's best for the baby and that basically the baby belongs with her," Schechter answered.

"All right now, Doctor," Abraham continued, "were there any other factors under 'narcissistic personality' that you considered?"

Schechter paused, leaned his shiny bald head toward the judge, and then whispered with a smile, "We discovered that Mrs. Whitehead was, indeed, Mrs. Whitehead. Her hair was totally white and she spent a good deal of time each week in dying her hair the color that it is because she felt this kept her more youthful-looking.

"It's a pattern that we're trying to develop," he explained, elaborating to the court during Harold Cassidy's cross-examination. "You see, she dyes her hair, and that's precisely related to this area of attempting to remain youthful and a preoccupation with grooming."

"How old is she, Doctor?" Cassidy asked, his voice soft and level.

"I believe twenty-seven. She's in the later part of her twenties." I was actually twenty-nine.

"You don't find it unusual," Cassidy continued, "that a woman who is in the later part of her twenties wouldn't want to walk around with shocks of white hair, do you?"

"Mr. Cassidy," Schechter said, "beauty is in the eye of the beholder. I happen to think that young faces with white hair are absolutely magnificent looking. Now that's my perception. Her perception is different. I'm not criticizing that this is what she does. I am merely stating that this is a factual piece of material which came out during our interviews."

When asked if he believed that my mixed personality disorder would continue indefinitely regardless of medical treatment, the doctor shook his head solemnly. "Yes," he said, "I do."

The cross-examination then turned to "schizotypal personality disorder," another category of mixed personality disorder. Searching among his papers, Schechter referred the court to the psychiatric manual he had used as his guide. "Under schizotypal personality disorder, page 313, DSM III, Capital A, number 1," he said, using his index finger as a marker, "you see, it includes magical thinking and bizarre fantasies or preoccupations." Schechter then told the court that the unusual expense of this trial was an example of the magical thinking typical of this disorder.

"Not only would they incur the expenses," he added, apparently in amazement, "they would take the rest of their lives to pay this off and continue on to the Supreme Court in case the New Jersey courts rule against them."

"And this has something to do with magical thinking?" Cassidy repeated, in an effort to clarify Schechter's position.

"It has to do with magical thinking, yes," Schechter answered, nodding emphatically.

"Doctor," Cassidy said, and then he paused. His voice became softer, his cadence slower, his gaze more intense. "How much money is too much money for Mrs. Whitehead to spend in order to win her child back?"

For a moment there was silence. "I think," Schechter finally said, ignoring Harold Cassidy's question and redirecting the dialogue, "everything that can be done within the scope of the law ought to be done to protect this child. It may," he added, "require termination of parental rights and then the permission of the courts for an adoption proceeding to take place."

Considering how closely this team of hired experts or "hit men," as Rick liked to call them, had worked together, it was not surprising that both Dr. Brodzinsky and Judith Greif's testimony mirrored that of Marshall Schechter. Though less extreme in their condemnation, they too claimed that, at least for a period of years, the baby would be better off without me.

When asked by Lorraine Abraham what he had observed about my relationship with the baby, Brodzinsky said, "We did see that she and the baby have an attachment relationship with one another. It affords this child some degree of security, a reasonable degree of security. Mrs. Whitehead was certainly the only individual in the Whitehead home toward which the baby showed discriminatory behavior. She sought out for specific purpose the mother as opposed to Mr. Whitehead or the children, or even us, for that matter.

"When she was stressed, she did show approach behavior toward the mother and was pretty easily comforted by Mrs. Whitehead. So I suggest that the attachment's there." He paused for a moment, and said, "There is no question in my mind that the attachment is there."

Nevertheless, Brodzinsky recommended that Sara and I be separated from each other for an indeterminate period of time because our contact would undermine Sara's relationship with the Sterns.

Like Brodzinsky, expert Judith Greif acknowledged Sara's attachment to me and said that she would have a strong need to know who I was. Yet she too recommended against contact because she thought I loved her too much. "The baby," said Greif, by way of explanation, "has become so special to her that she in some way has fused with the child."

Now and then, there is, in the public's perception, the sense that witnesses have gone so far in an effort to discredit a litigant that they have actually discredited themselves and, to a lesser degree, the professions they represent.

There was without question something in the testimony for which each of these experts requested $12,000, particularly the testimony of Marshall Schechter, that offended the people. As a result, the backlash that had begun when Lee Salk called me a surrogate uterus now took on larger proportions.

"Dr. Marshall Schechter, Professor Emeritus of Child Psychiatry at the University of Pennsylvania, has firm ideas about the right and wrong way to play patty-cake," wrote Russell Baker in *The New York Times* a few days after Schechter completed his testimony:

> "The wrong way," he testified at the Baby M custody trial in Hackensack, New Jersey, "is to say hooray when the kid claps her hands together. The right way? When the baby claps, the grownup should imitate the action and clap back while saying patty-cake." . . . As an expert witness he urged the judge to end Mrs. Whitehead's parental rights in order "to protect this child." He didn't like Mrs. Whitehead having four stuffed pandas for the baby to play with either. In the play department, Dr. Schechter is a kitchenware man. "Pots, pans and spoons would have been more suitable than pandas," he testified. Now if the courts heed the experts, she could end up without even the right to see the baby.

After dinner, I read Russell Baker's column out loud to Rick as we sat at the kitchen table. I laughed in spite of myself, then turned to Rick and said, "It's really not funny."

"Don't worry about it. Look, here's another one, Mary," Rick said cheerfully as he began quoting Richard Cohen, another syndicated columnist, who summed up the report by writing, "Doctor Marshall Schechter, the psychiatrist who testified against the surrogate mother, has inadvertently performed something of a public service in rendering such foolish judgment against Mary Beth Whitehead. He has both caricatured his profession and highlighted the increasing tendency to subject parenting to something that pretends to be scientific analysis."

"Don't worry about it," Rick repeated when he saw that I had stopped laughing. "This guy Schechter helped you. He actually helped you."

I was especially sensitive because I was so worn out

from the long, grueling days at court. Since Rick had to be at work by five, my parents had come up from Florida to get the kids off to school. Rick was usually asleep by the time I got back from court, so we barely saw each other. When we were together we rarely talked about the case; we were finding it too painful to deal with. We had begun to drift apart and live in our separate worlds. We weren't fighting, we just weren't communicating.

I had been getting up at five-thirty each morning and leaving the house at six-thirty in order to get to court on time. I was usually too rushed for breakfast. My weekly visitations with the baby had been scheduled during the lunch hour so that the Sterns wouldn't have to miss any time in court. On the days when I saw her, I missed lunch as well. On one of those days before I had returned from my visit with Sara, the court bailiff led Sue Hergenhan to the stand.

Back in April of 1984, this delicate, fine-featured woman who had been my neighbor and closest friend for three and a half years had been badly injured in an ice-skating accident and had broken both of her arms at the elbows. For two months she needed complete care. She had to be fed and bathed. Her teeth had to be brushed, her nose had to be blown. She also needed someone to help take care of her two young children and take over her job in the family's swimming pool business.

Each morning at seven I came over with Tuesday and Ryan. First we'd all eat breakfast together. Then I'd get the kids off to school. After that I'd dress Sue and do her housework and the scheduling and banking for the family business. Then I'd do the cooking. Rick would come over and eat dinner with us. At eight o'clock he would take my kids home to do their homework. I'd stay on until eleven and come home after getting Sue to bed.

Even though it was a hard routine, I enjoyed helping her. It's the kind of thing I've always been best at. Sue felt that she could never adequately repay me. That, unfortunately, led us to another terrible problem.

It began when Sue was questioned on the witness stand about May 5. First, I am told, she described the horror of that day and her own frantic attempts to help. "I was in my house and I heard screaming coming from Mary's yard," she explained. "I told my children to stay in the house and I went over to her yard. In the yard I saw Mary holding the baby. Clutching the baby. There were two police officers with their arms on her. Betsy, Bill, and Rick were in the yard. Tuesday was running around the yard screaming, 'Don't take my baby sister, take me instead. Leave my mother alone. Leave my father alone.' She was hysterical, crying. She just hung on to Mary. She wouldn't let go of her. She was afraid her mother was going to be taken away with the baby."

"Did you know subsequently whether Mary Beth Whitehead went to Florida?" Gary Skoloff asked.

"Yes. I know that she went," Sue replied.

"Did she ever call you when she was in Florida?"

"Yes, she did," Sue said. "She called me and said that they were fine. They were all down in Florida. She didn't tell me where she was. . . ."

Skoloff looked suspicious. "Did she call you again, after that?"

"Yes," Sue said, "she did."

"When was that?" Skoloff pressed.

"A couple of days after she was trying to get a lawyer," Sue answered. "She was having great difficulty in obtaining a lawyer in Florida."

"Did she ask you to help her?"

"Yes, she did."

"Were you able to?"

"No, I wasn't."

"What did you do, or try to do?"

"My father's a lawyer," Sue explained, "so I called him. He called a few lawyers and spoke with another neighbor of mine who made calls to lawyers. No one was interested. . . ."

Then Gary Skoloff approached the witness stand and asked Sue if she had ever read the May 5 court order. Sue hesitated, and shifted nervously in her seat. "No," she said finally, "I didn't." Sue was dismissed. As soon as I returned from my visit with Sara, I was called to the stand.

"Mrs. Whitehead," Skoloff said with an excited edge to his voice, "do you recollect sending a letter to Judge Harvey Sorkow?"

"No, I don't," I answered. As the questioning continued, I vaguely remembered a telephone conversation with Sue, when I was in hiding in Florida, in which she suggested writing a letter to the judge for me, explaining why we had run away. But in the months of confusion that followed, we had never talked about it again; it simply hadn't come up.

Now, as Gary Skoloff questioned me, the judge joined in. His face turned red, his voice rose in anger. "It seems that somebody may be playing fast and loose with the court," he thundered as he called for a recess.

Sue ran up to me in the hallway. "Mary," she said, "that's my letter, and I did see that court paper on your lawn the day the police were there."

Seeing how frightened she looked, I hugged her.

"Don't worry about it, Sue," I said. "I'll explain it to the judge. It'll be all right."

Sue had often written letters for me to the school on Ryan's behalf, simply because she was better at it than I was. We'd always helped each other in whatever ways we could. We were like sisters. She could express my feelings perfectly, because she understood them.

When the trial resumed, Gary Skoloff handed me the letter. I looked at it. "When the police arrived to seize the baby from my breast," it said, "we were helpless and trapped. We had no alternative other than to do what we did. Now we have left our home, possessions and my husband's job, and we cannot as yet find a lawyer who will take our case. I am still trying and I will succeed. I will not let our happiness be destroyed. We will remain a family, with our daughter, Sara, a well-cared-for and loved member."

"Have you ever seen this?" Skoloff asked.

"No, I've never seen it," I answered. "But I can explain."

"But you can explain," Skoloff mimicked as he waved his arms in the air.

"Yes, I can," I said.

"You'd better explain!" Sorkow shouted from the bench.

"I've just talked to Sue, sir, and she wrote it," I stammered.

"Who?" the judge roared.

"Sue Hergenhan. She wrote it on my behalf. She just told me."

"Sue wrote it on your behalf," the judge repeated incredulously. "When did you find out?"

"She just told me," I said, nodding and swallowing hard.

With a gesture of disgust that went beyond words, Sorkow dismissed me and called Sue back to the stand.

She was terrified that they would throw her in jail. But she knew that if she didn't tell the truth, I would look like a liar. So she admitted to writing the letter.

"Did you understand," Skoloff continued, "that when Judge Sorkow received that letter he would think he was receiving a letter directly from Mary Beth Whitehead?"

"Yes," she answered timidly.

"And didn't you testify on the stand several hours ago that you'd never seen any of the court documents?" Skoloff asked, knowing that Sue had referred to the May 5 court order in her letter.

"Yes, I did," she acknowledged.

"Was that a truthful statement?"

"No, it wasn't," Sue managed.

"You knowingly made an untruthful statement to the court under oath?" Sorkow shouted incredulously from the bench.

"Yes," Sue answered, her voice barely audible.

"You know," Sorkow said, pouncing on her admission like a hungry lion, "I have no alternative but to consult with the prosecutor on this."

Sue nodded sadly as Sorkow threw his hands in the air, like a man so disgusted that he had nothing else to say.

An hour after court adjourned, prosecutor Larry J. McClure announced that his staff would study the findings and, if necessary, present them to a grand jury. If found guilty of perjury, he said, Sue could be sentenced to five years in prison and a $15,000 fine.

As it turned out, no action was ever taken against her—probably because, as Harold Cassidy later explained to me, when somebody has given a statement that is inaccurate and takes the opportunity to correct it, it is not perjury.

Nevertheless, the next day, newspaper headlines announced, PERJURY PROBE: WITNESS FOR WHITEHEAD ADMITS FORGING LETTER AND LYING UNDER OATH. As well intentioned as she was, Sue Hergenhan had inadvertently given the court one more thing to hold against me.

As the weeks passed, the proceedings became so painful that I gradually withdrew. First I began sitting in a room with the guards. I felt drained and numb and as tired as I had felt during the first few months of my pregnancy with Sara. I didn't want to expose myself to more punishment. I wanted to be with my other two children. Finally, I started staying at home for several days at a time.

Bill Stern and Rick had also stopped coming to court. Rick, who couldn't afford the time off, had stopped first, then Bill said he, too, had used up all of his vacation time. During most of the last two weeks, just Betsy Stern attended. One day, even she was gone, leaving only the lawyers to argue among themselves.

The first day I returned to court, I was touched by the sight of dozens of women demonstrating outside the courtroom. Some were carrying signs that said MOTHERS WITH FEELINGS. They represented a group of women who had decided to support me publicly. Others, from the New Jersey Citizens Against Surrogate Parenting, were also there.

"This case is about a baby being torn from its mother's arms," Michelle Harrison, an obstetrician and psychiatrist who had helped to organize the demonstration, told the press. "The court has taken away Mary Beth's baby. Expert witnesses have questioned her abilities to mother, saying that she should have bought pots and pans, not a panda, for Sara. And that she's an unfit mother because she doesn't play patty-cake right. On those terms, my own children could be taken from me. If this could be done to her, it could happen to anyone.

"I don't normally read press reports and jump onto planes to protest," Harrison added. "But I've agonized over what Mary Beth is going through and the court's distortion of it. She's done nothing but commit herself to loving and raising her child."

"Thank you," I said to Harrison as I walked past the reporters and held out my hand. "What you're doing is very moving. It helps me to know that people are behind me."

On the last day of testimony, the Vatican itself issued a scathing statement that condemned all forms of artificial fertilization and surrogacy. It also asked government leaders to impose "moral" controls on these activities.

Although the Church did not take a specific stand on my case, I was gratified to see surrogacy opposed and the basic concept of the child's right to be with her biological mother supported. I was also relieved to think that the anguish and pain of the trial were finally going to end.

# Chapter **15**

# Closing Arguments

Mrs. Whitehead descended into a public hell of exposure and humiliation to try to keep her child. This forced us all to face surrogate motherhood as an issue that touched our own beliefs and souls. For that she deserved respect, perhaps even a touch of gratitude, certainly not a judge's vilification.

> —A. M. Rosenthal in *The New York Times*, May 5, 1987

**T**he eight-week trial had taken a heavy toll on my life and my strength. As we walked through deep snow and ice on the final day, sliding against the reporters who surrounded us like maggots, I was so cold and so weary that I could barely keep my balance.

I sat quietly in the front row of the courtroom, feeling as if I had been frozen in the blizzard outside, and listened numbly as one of the attorneys tried to convince the judge that even if my rights were terminated, Sara should be allowed to see my mother and father since they were her only living grandparents.

When it came time for Harold Cassidy to make his closing argument, he seemed calm. He spoke softly, as if he was making a last conciliatory attempt to dispel the judge's anger. Sorkow stared straight ahead without expression when Cassidy reminded the court that I had never signed relinquishment papers, because from the moment of the baby's birth, I had known that I could not surrender her.

After summarizing the events that had occurred between Sara's birth and my flight to Florida, Cassidy glanced briefly at his notes, then turned to the judge and said, "Your Honor, Bill Stern's before the court now, asking you to terminate the rights of Mrs. Whitehead. But what is the justification for the proposed sentence of a lifetime of suffering? . . . The justification in essence is that he received a promise from Mrs. Whitehead, upon which he alleges he relied. But Mr. Stern testified during this trial that he actually did *not* rely upon that promise at all. He testified that when he signed the agreement, he did not think that if the surrogate mother did not voluntarily surrender the baby, he could go to court and make her give the child to him. He actually *knew* in advance that he couldn't legally rely upon the agreement, that it was truly the option of Mrs. Whitehead to either retain custody or not to retain custody."

Cassidy reminded Judge Sorkow of the report from Dr. Joan Einwohner, at the New York Infertility Center, which said that I would probably not be able to relinquish my baby. Then he added gravely, "There is something uniquely cruel about determining by a psychiatric examination that a woman is incapable of surrendering a child following birth, and going forward with the artificial insemination of the woman anyway."

Cassidy recalled my mistaken belief that Betsy was infertile. "Childbearing would have been an inconvenience for Mrs. Stern. . . . The risk of paralysis with her particular condition was no greater than the risk to the general population. All of the medical witnesses testified that multiple sclerosis does not prevent conception and that there is little impact, if any, on the course and outcome of pregnancy. . . . In truth, the risk of death to Mrs. Stern was no greater then the risk of death to Mrs. Whitehead. . . . Infertility was a lie. Inconvenience was the truth.

"And so it was that Mrs. Whitehead, who was motivated to help an infertile couple, to assist in giving the gift of life, was impregnated. Even though it was clear to anyone who bothered to read Joan Einwohner's report that she probably would not be able to surrender the child and carry out the transfer of custody, which would have sentenced her to a lifetime of suffering."

Cassidy paused. His eyes met mine. There was a look of friendship and genuine concern.

"Enforcement of such an agreement would be contrary to everything our public policy stands for," he said, this time looking directly at the judge. "The only basis for such a transfer and termination requires a showing of actual abandonment or abuse of the child. In the absence of any such showing, there can be no compelled transfer or termination. . . . We must never permit a man to have one woman to share his life and another to experience the sacrifice and pain of pregnancy. . . . The truth is—the bottom line is—that Mrs. Stern did not read a psychological report because Mrs. Stern thought her career was too important to bear her own children. That can never be a reason for us to abandon our carefully enunciated public policies. . . . That cannot be the basis for setting a historical precedent of taking a child from her mother. . . . That's why this case is bigger than Mary Beth Whitehead. It's bigger than William Stern. Mary Beth Whitehead has tried this case for all surrogate mothers.

"What we are witnessing, and what we can predict will happen, is that one class of Americans will exploit another class. And it will always be the wife of the sanitation worker who must bear the children for the pediatrician.

"The truth is," Cassidy said with gravity and intensity, "that she is guilty of certain things. She is guilty of fear. The fear that she would never see her child again. The fear that she would be forced to live without her baby for the rest of her life. She is also guilty of some acts that resulted out of that fear. For instance, she is guilty of disobeying the court order."

Once more Cassidy paused, and when he resumed, his voice was even softer, his cadence slower than before. "I guess that, in reality, she's guilty of loving her baby too much as well. Because she did some things out of love and out of fear that later would be used against her.

"But," he said, leaning forward and seeming almost to whisper, "what she did was the only option because the bottom line is that, above all, Mary Beth Whitehead is a mother, and without that she is nothing in this life."

The sadness in his voice, the softness of his tone, had a weight to it that seemed to hush the courtroom. Every eye was on him, and many were filled with tears. Even Judge Sorkow looked uncomfortable as he shifted in his seat.

In what seemed like an effort to break the spell that Cassidy had created, Gary Skoloff immediately asked the judge to depart from normal protocol. "Your Honor, may we have a five-minute recess?" he said.

"No break, no break," Sorkow snapped irritably.

"I need three minutes at the men's room, Judge,"

Skoloff quipped. "Three cups of coffee this morning," he added, raising his eyebrows and forcing a laugh. "I'm not going to make it."

At that point, I too got up and walked quietly out of Judge Sorkow's courtroom for the last time. I was finally leaving behind the marble halls and domed ceilings that seemed to substitute formality for justice. Outside, several dozen women stood in the snow carrying signs that said SARA IS A LITTLE SISTER; SARA WHITEHEAD IS HER NAME; and WOMEN ARE NOT DOGS FOR BREEDING. They distributed a statement that had been signed by more than one hundred prominent women, including Betty Friedan, Gloria Steinem, Nora Ephron, Susan Sontag, Meryl Streep, Sally Quinn, Margaret Atwood, Andrea Dworkin, and Hunter College president Donna Shalala. The statement quoted the experts who had condemned me and then said, "By these standards we are all unfit mothers. . . . There are increasingly complex questions of custody today—both in cases involving surrogate parents and those involving divorce— and we strongly urge the legislators and jurists who will deal with these matters to recognize that a mother need not be perfect to 'deserve' her child."

Marilyn French, author of *A Women's Room*, had voiced her own reaction. She said, "It is like the whole middle-class world is standing with arms clasped against this poor woman who dared to open her mouth and say 'I want my baby.' "

I stopped to thank the women and to shake their hands, but I began to cry when someone started chanting, "Bring that baby home."

Then, as the snow fell, a woman walked over and put her arms around me. Suddenly, everyone began to sing "That's What Friends Are For." As I stood there comforted by these strangers who were my friends, for the first time in many weeks, I wept.

I did not return to Judge Sorkow's courtroom that afternoon to hear Gary Skoloff's closing argument. But, as I had expected, the report in *The New York Times* confirmed that it was "a blistering attack" in which Skoloff repeatedly branded me "a liar," and claimed that the Sterns had become "victims of a plot." "The bottom line," Skoloff argued, "is simple. You cannot believe anything the Whiteheads tell you. They lie."

Lorraine Abraham, on the other hand, had surprised the press by "only" urging a separation of several years. She recommended that my parental rights be retained; she claimed that terminating them would be both "irrevocable" and "inhuman." She said, "To now sit in judgment and project the needs of this child in the future is not something anyone who has appeared on this stand can do with any degree of professional probability. . . . Termination now is so awesome a step that we cannot in all conscience take it. We are not omniscient."

# Chapter 16

# The Birthday Gift

Rumpelstiltskin is a very old fairy tale by the Brothers Grimm. . . . The beautiful but poor miller's daughter promises the dwarf to give him her first-born child if he will spin gold out of straw for her.

Rumpelstiltskin agrees. "The Gold is spun, the child is born. Now give me what you promised me," the dwarf demands.

The girl weeps. "I love my child!"

"A deal is a deal," says the dwarf. The girl weeps some more.

The story ends happily. . . . It would seem that even the little dwarf, Rumpelstiltskin, had more compassion in his heart for the plight of a mother than the harsh and unrelenting judgment of the court in the case of Baby M.

—Stella K. Hershan in *The New York Times*, April 4, 1987 (letter to the editor)

**B**efore he lowered the ax, Judge Sorkow granted us one last wish: the right to see Sara on her first birthday. As a stipulation, however, the judge ruled that the meeting would be held in a secret place to avoid press coverage. Since I couldn't be trusted, I was not allowed to know where the meeting would be. My attorneys were ordered to keep the spot a secret.

I wanted desperately to see her. And I wanted Rick and the children to see her, but I had mixed feelings. I was tired of the games and I didn't know if I could handle the pain of thinking that we were saying good-bye for the last time. The kids, on the other hand, were so excited and grateful that they acted as if Harvey Sorkow were Santa Claus.

Tuesday wrapped the presents in panda wrapping paper, which I had bought in one of my feistier moments in response to Schechter's comment that I should have given the baby pots and pans, not pandas, to play with. There was a wind-up toy radio that played "Over the Rainbow," a set of plastic beads, a Fisher-Price toy piano, and a plastic shopping cart. Tuesday and I also baked a huge tray of cupcakes and iced them with chocolate. We were in one of my attorneys' cars, speeding toward our secret destination, before the attorney was permitted to tell us that we were going to Lorraine Abraham's house.

I would rather have had the party in a prison cell. Still, it was wonderful to see all of my children together, unwrapping gifts and playing. Sara, who was just learning to walk, would take a step or two, then fall onto our laps. We played and took pictures in the yard for a while. When we came in, it hit me that we only had five or ten minutes left before the sheriff's officers would arrive to take her away again. I cried and held her in my arms and kissed her. I pressed my cheek against hers and closed my eyes, trying to make the moment last.

"Your mommy loves you," I whispered as the sheriff's cars arrived. "Your mommy loves you," I repeated as they took her from my arms.

# Chapter 17

# Termination of My Parental Rights

The Baby M case was a tragedy without a villain until the very end, and then the judge stepped forward.

His logic was flawed, his sense of mercy nonexistent. He used his power not only to take a child away from its mother, but to keep them from ever seeing each other again. He denounced the mother needlessly and brutally. He exploited the judge's position on the bench.

> —A. M. Rosenthal in *The New York Times*,
> April 5, 1987

**I**t was March 31, 1987, and raining like a monsoon. Pouring, pelting, horrible rain that flooded the roads, leaving them blocked and flowing like rivers. But the weather didn't stop the press. More than two hundred reporters, photographers, and TV technicians from as far away as Japan, Sweden, Great Britain, South America, and the Soviet Union converged on the courthouse.

Judge Sorkow was scheduled to announce his decision at 1:00 P.M. Security was so tight that spectators, and even reporters with press passes, had to go through metal detectors. Police blocked all of the exits and entrances to the courthouse. Cameras were not allowed inside, so scores of cameramen and photographers milled about outside in the rain while Judge Sorkow spent three hours and five minutes reading his 121-page opinion. We all knew that I was about to be massacred. Preferring to receive the punishment in private, I had remained at home, but people who were there told me in detail what happened. First, Sorkow recounted the histories of each of our families. He spoke of the connection between the Sterns and me, and of my refusal to surrender the baby. He referred to each of the experts' reports and then, as reporters yawned and looked at their watches, he finally got to his own opinion.

"The court," he said evenly, "is satisfied that . . . Mrs. Whitehead is manipulative, impulsive, and exploitative. She is also for the most part untruthful, choosing only to remember what may enhance her position, or altering the facts about which she is testifying or intentionally not remembering. . . . The judgment-making ability of Mrs. Whitehead is sorely tested."

As he continued, Harvey Sorkow's mouth began to tremble and his face grew flushed. "She is a woman without empathy. . . . She expresses none for her husband's problems with alcohol, and her infusion of her other children into this process, exposing them rather than protecting them from the searing scrutiny of the media, mitigates against her claim for custody.

"It is," he continued with his voice rising, "for all these reasons . . . that we find, by clear and convincing evidence, indeed by a measure of evidence reaching beyond reasonable doubt, that Melissa's best interests will be served by being placed in her father's sole custody. . . . Enforcing the contract will leave Mr. and Mrs. Whitehead in the same position that they were in when the contract was made. To not enforce the contract will give them the child and deprive Mr. Stern of his promised benefits. This court therefore will specifically enforce the surrogate-parenting agreement to compel delivery of the child to the father and terminate the mother's parental rights."

Reporters, who until this point had been waiting impatiently for the bottom line, gasped collectively. No one, not even the Sterns, had expected the judge to go this far. At last they had what they needed. Many reporters ran from the courtroom to the telephones, cameras, and typewriters outside.

"He upheld the contract!" someone shouted. "The baby's going to the Sterns."

"She's terminated!" another yelled.

Inside, Judge Sorkow continued to read. He said that my parents, too, would be "terminated." He called them "unworthy" of the "benefit and relief" they sought from the court. Then, for a moment, Sorkow stopped reading and looked slowly around the courtroon. His eyes stopped at the defense table. "It felt," Harold Cassidy's co-counsel Robert Ruggieri recalled later, "as if he was growling at us, his face was beet red, his jowls were shaking, and he was really worked into a lather. It was wild to watch so much hatred."

"The parental rights of the defendant, Mary Beth Whitehead, are terminated," he roared as he reached the grand crescendo of his speech. "Mr. Stern is formally judged the father of Melissa Stern. The New Jersey Department of Health, Bureau of Vital Statistics . . . is directed to amend all records of birth to reflect his paternity, and the name of the child is to be Melissa Stern."

Minutes after he finished his last sentence, Harvey Sorkow took Bill and Betsy Stern into his chambers. And in an unprecendented act that burned me like acid, he conducted an instant adoption ceremony and told the world that Betsy Stern was now my baby's legal mother.

Reporters swarmed all over my front lawn. But I was alone in the basement, quietly and methodically folding my laundry, when one of Harold's partners came downstairs. I was as prepared as I could ever be.

"Mary," Roger Foss said gently, "the news is so terrible that it's wonderful. It exposes the extent of the judge's bias. It will never stand up. We'll appeal it immediately."

Only after that preface did he tell me that all of my rights had been terminated, meaning that if the judge's ruling was upheld, I would never see Sara again. Finally he added that Besty had already adopted the baby. First I finished folding the laundry and then I walked back upstairs to face my children. That was the hardest part.

"She's not coming home today," I said softly. "It will take a little bit longer."

"Don't worry, Mom," Tuesday said, taking my hand. "She's coming home, we know it. We feel it."

Later that night, Robert Ruggieri came to see me and provide emotional support. We talked for hours. He explained that Sorkow's decision was contrary to the body of law throughout the entire world. He said that the enforcement of the surrogate parenting contract was indecent and the worst form of exploitation.

"Mary," he added, "have faith. Believe me, your case is going to decide public policy in this state and ultimately in this country. Sorkow has ruled that surrogate parenting is a constitutionally protected activity, and he's wrong."

At eleven-thirty that night, Harold Cassidy appeared on "Nightline" with Gary Skoloff and Ted Koppel.

"What are all these appeals about? Isn't it time to end

all this and accept the judge's ruling?" Koppel asked, implying, to my distress, that even he thought I had had my day in court and justice had been rendered.

"No, Mr. Koppel," Harold answered firmly, "it isn't. The legal analysis was flawed and incorrect. To stop now would be a disservice to the human race. You will see. There will be a reversal."

"I will not give up," I said at a press conference in Red Bank the next afternoon. "I will fight as long as it takes. She's my flesh and blood. No judge can change that. There can never be a court-appointed termination of my love for Sara. We will not accept the decision of one judge as the final determination of a whole society, that we should be permanently separated. I believe that there is something so wrong and so harmfully unnatural about the surrogate practice that our courts will return Sara to me."

The next day, in another show of support, more than fifty feminists picketed in front of the New York Infertility Center, carrying signs that said SORKOW THE TERMINATOR and A ONE-NIGHT STAND IN A DISH DOESN'T MAKE A MAN A FATHER.

"The entire trial was a farce," Dr. Phyllis Chesler added with bitter intensity. "It was a gang rape. A public daily crucifixion of a perfectly good mother."

To my amazement, feminists from all over the country were now vowing to create a mass movement against surrogate motherhood, condemning the practice as reproductive prostitution and a form of involuntary servitude for women. They called Noel Keane a "pimp" and pledged to close his business. "We are here for Mary Beth Whitehead to tell her that we admire her courage," one of them said.

Later in the afternoon, messages from feminists around the world were read to reporters. Maria Mies of Germany said, "We are horrified that an American judge can take away the human right of a mother to the child born of her, a right recognized by people since time immemorial, and replace it with the law of the market, the law of the contract."

"We feel revolted and angry," a feminist from France added.

"The last time in our country," said Dr. Michelle Harrison, "that we allowed the breeding of human beings for the transfer of ownership was during slavery. Isn't having a baby seized and losing parental rights like being raped? Is rape too extreme a description? Most women would rather be raped than give up one of their children. So maybe to call it rape minimizes what has been done to this mother, this child. Maybe the more appropriate language is the one of slavery, of bondage; of mothers, fathers, and children being sold away. Maybe it's more like the cries of mothers and children taken from each other in the name of creating the perfect race. We have been there too recently."

Three days later, the Supreme Court of New Jersey announced that it had accepted our case and would hear the arguments in September. Pending our appeal, they also restored my visitation rights. However, they cut the time in half, saying that I could now only see Sara for two hours, *once* a week.

# Chapter 18

# The Slow Path of Emotional Recovery

From the ashes of Sara Whitehead, Melissa Stern was born.

—Michelle Harrison, M.D., in
*Southern Feminist*, Summer 1987

**D**espite my public show of confidence, I no longer felt sure that Sara would ever be able to come home. Without that belief, my life seemed meaningless.

I was still trying to function. In fact, I was scrubbing the floors harder and vacuuming the rugs even after they were spotless. I was ironing the kids' T-shirts and underwear and cooking bigger and more elaborate dinners. But the mechanical activities no longer helped. I felt as if part of me had died with the lost dream of Sara.

As the month of April drew to a close, I realized that the old feelings of grief, self-hatred, and worthlessness, which I had experienced when I let the Sterns take the baby home the first time, had returned. There were days when my chest ached as if my heart had ruptured inside me.

The rockslide of emotions was hurting everyone close to me. No one could reach me. Rick no longer knew how to comfort me. It seemed as if somehow, in losing the fight for Sara we had also lost each other. Now, when we tried to reach out, all we could feel was the pain of our shared failure.

As the days passed, my manic bursts of energy were becoming less and less frequent. Cleaning and cooking no longer distracted me. I began to stay inside my house for days on end. Sometimes I lacked the energy even to get dressed. Instead, I would sit and look at Sara's photograph and cry as if I were experiencing the loss for the first time. If I couldn't be her mother, I wanted nothing from life and I had nothing to give it. When Peggy Karcher, the wife of one of my attorneys, arrived one afternoon to find me crying and still in my bathrobe at three o'clock, she decided I needed a change.

Peggy and Alan Karcher owned a condominium in St. Thomas. She said it was a wonderful place to rest and come alive again. On May 5, 1987, the anniversary of our first confrontation with the police, we took the cheapest flight, with a five-hour layover in Puerto Rico. On the way down, the only thing I could think about was my lost baby, but Peggy was right about St. Thomas. All my life I had lived near water and loved it. But I had never seen any place that was as beautiful as this. The palm trees, blue water, and white sand made me feel as if I had entered a different world.

Day after day I lay in the sun. The warmer I got, the better I liked it. I had been so cold and numb for so long. Over and over I listened to the sound of the waves crashing against the shore. As they came and left and then returned again, dozens of images of joy and sorrow, of loving Sara and losing her, came and went with them.

As the days passed I became so satiated with the rhythm of distance and return that slowly, inexplicably, I began to hope again. I started to believe once more that my connection with Sara was also immutable, that our love would always return. The bond had been severed by the Sterns and Judge Sorkow, but it could never really be broken.

With that belief, I started to recover my stability and energy and to gain a new level of inner strength. I began to reenter the world and enjoy the beauty around me. A dog's footprint in the sand, a seagull circling above me. Even the sight of a sunburned child, who looked like Sara, comforted me. For the first time in many months, I was at peace. I felt released from the despair that had immobilized me, and somehow freer than ever to pursue new possibilities.

My first sun-drenched image of Dean Gould was of a tall, athletic young man with a boyish grin and a velvet voice. He smiled and asked if my sunburn hurt. I didn't yet know it, but my knight in corduroy shorts and Adidas sneakers had just stepped out of a rented Jeep. He was with a group of his friends and I was with Peggy. We all stood around making small talk for a while. Then, as Peggy and I were about to leave, Dean pointed at a restaurant on the beach and said, "How about all of us going to dinner at the Bird Cage?" The others agreed.

I looked hesitantly at Peggy. She grinned and nodded with emphatic enthusiasm. Afterward, we all piled into the Jeep. As the hilly roads threw us together, I accidentally touched Dean's leg. I drew back my hand as if it had been burned, and suddenly I knew there was something about my reaction to him that I had never experienced before. I laughed awkwardly and we kept driving. The next curve was so sharp that he actually had to grab me and hold on to my arm to keep me from falling out of the Jeep. That was the first of many times that Dean Gould saved me.

Our friends decided to go for a midnight swim. Dean and I ended up sitting on the beach and talking. I learned that he was a twin who had worked his way through college as a short-order cook. Now, at twenty-six, he was a Wall Street accountant. Still unmarried, he lived with his mother and father in the modest Long Island neighborhood where he had grown up. When I told Dean who I was, he said my notoriety didn't matter. He was more concerned about the fact that I was married than that I was the mother of Baby M.

From Thursday night to Saturday night we never slept and we never left each other's side. By midnight on Friday, we were both completely exhausted but still unwilling to sleep. We knew that our time together was running out. As we walked up and down the dock, looking at beautiful yachts under a full moon, Dean told me that although he knew I was married and had two children at home, he had feelings for me that he hadn't ever thought possible. He kissed me and said he'd been looking for me all his life.

I had never met anyone like Dean before. In fact, Rick was the only man I had ever dated. In spite of his reassurances, I didn't know if I'd ever see Dean again. He told me he would call me, and I wanted to believe him, but there had been so many disappointments in the last year that I was afraid. Feeling depressed and defensive, I watched Dean board a bus for the airport, then turned and walked away as quickly as possible, without allowing myself to look back.

But Dean did call—again and again. "You're the magnet and I'm the steel," he said, laughing, when we finally met in a bustling New York restaurant. Still, things were nothing like they'd been in St. Thomas. I was with my family again, and seeing Dean was almost worse than not seeing him. The meetings were so short, so public, and so guilt-ridden. The partings were so difficult that most of the time we just talked on the phone. By June 28, when my children left for eight weeks of summer camp, Dean and I knew we had to spend some time together. Dean moved out of his parents' home and rented a one-bedroom apartment on the top floor of a Victorian house in Summit, New Jersey.

I told Rick as gently as I could that I had met another man. Even in the agony of the first shock and the anger and wrenching pain of pulling apart, Rick and I never lost our respect or love for each other. Nothing, even the grief of no longer relating as husband and wife, could change the fact that we shared two children and many beautiful times together.

For fifteen years, many people, even some of my own family, had been telling me that Rick was a poor provider, that he would never change, and that I should leave him. Rick knew this and had always been deeply troubled by our financial problems. The trial had further demeaned him. Now, by the press and the world, he had been characterized as "an alcoholic garbageman." But Richard Whitehead will always be one of the best and kindest and gentlest men I have ever known. Nothing made me more certain of that than the dignity with which he let me go.

"I love you, Mary," he whispered as we sat on the living room couch, crying, with our arms around each other. I think deep down he knew that I wasn't coming back. "Take as long as you need," he said. "I'll be waiting here for you if you decide to come home."

Summit is a conservative town, halfway between my home in Bricktown and the Conklin Center where I visited Sara. Hiding behind sunglasses and a French braid, I wandered anonymously, passing the long afternoons among its antique shops, gourmet food stores, and churches, often feeling very empty and alone and pining for my children. In the evenings I'd meet Dean at the train station, we'd cook quiet dinners, and I'd lie in his arms, where, somehow, I always found comfort and peace.

On one such day I returned home feeling so faint that I could hardly hold my head up. When my back began to ache and my fever jumped to 102, I knew it was a recurrence of the kidney infection I had experienced in Florida. I called Dean at work and told him I was driving to the emergency room.

He said, "Wait, I'll come home and take you."

"No," I answered. "I'm too sick to wait." I spent the next six days at the Overlook Hospital in Summit. Then I left on Tuesday morning, although I still wasn't completely well, because I couldn't bear to miss my weekly visit with Sara. Each Tuesday I would emerge from my seclusion just long enough for the precious but wrenching two-hour guarded visit. The press would always be waiting to photograph me as I arrived and left, accompanied by a sheriff's officer.

My attorneys were urging me to return to Rick. They felt that the separation would damage my case, which was scheduled to be heard before the Supreme Court on September 14.

"I can't," I told Harold with passionate singlemindedness. "I just can't. This is something I have to do for myself."

Finally, early in August, Harold wrote a letter to the Supreme Court telling them that Rick and I had separated. After that, we released a statement to the press. The lawyers for the Sterns were jubilant. They issued a public statement that said, "During the course of the trial, we submitted proofs indicating that the Whitehead family suffered from instability and particularly marital friction. What we've just learned confirms those proofs." Actually, I was still going back and forth to Bricktown, cleaning and cooking for Rick and spending as much time as I could with him. My time with Dean had such a storybook quality that I wanted to make sure that what I was feeling was real and what I was doing was right.

Each time I saw Rick, the core of the problem became clearer. We had emerged from the public humiliation and character assassination of the trial feeling like two gutter rats who had no right to be in the world, let alone raise a baby. When we were together, those feelings returned. I was still very torn about leaving Rick, but I had come to grips with the reality that the trial had changed both of our lives. In many ways I was simply a different person, and I could no longer help Rick or myself by staying. Each time I was reunited with Dean, I found new strength. Dean made me feel like a person, whole and alive again. I was enriched and enhanced by our love. Not only did it renew me, but it carried me beyond the boundaries of myself and helped me to move forward.

I began to grow deeply interested in the plight of other surrogate mothers and in the broader legal and ethical implications of surrogacy. I decided that if I could help prevent other women from going through what I had experienced, my struggle and my loss would not be meaningless.

While Dean was away at work, I started to spend more and more of my free time focusing on the issue of surrogacy. I was in contact with women from all over the country. I learned of Allejandra Munoz, a young, illiterate Mexican woman who had been brought into America illegally in order to serve as a surrogate for distant relatives. After signing a contract she could not read, Allejandra says she was kept a virtual prisoner inside the house while the sperm donor's wife walked around with a small pillow under her maternity clothing.

When Allejandra told the couple that she could not go through with the arrangement and wanted to keep her baby, she says they threatened to turn her over to immigration authorities. After the child's birth, it took her three months to find a lawyer and collect $700 for a retainer. During that time she had never been permitted to see the child.

In February of 1987 she was granted the right to remain in this country for a year at a time. A judge also ordered visitation privileges, but her child still lives with the father. It took an additional year before her daughter was allowed to stay with her one night a week.

Under the court's latest ruling, the couple has the baby every night and on weekends. Allejandra takes care of her during the day, Monday through Thursday, while the husband and wife go to work. As is so often the case, the couple has a nice house, money, and education. They are professionals. By comparison, Allejandra is poor and powerless.

I agreed to go to Washington with Allejandra and several other women, to testify at congressional hearings. I had also accepted invitations to speak at the Harvard

Law School and to lend my support to organizations dedicated to fighting surrogacy. I didn't fully understand it yet, but in the process of helping others I was also healing myself.

As the end of August approached, I knew I had to say good-bye to Dean. My children were returning from camp, and as much as I loved Dean, my priority was to be there for them.

My parting with Dean may have been even harder on him than it was on me. I, at least, was distracted by the joyous return of Tuesday and Ryan, by the work of getting them ready for school, and by my growing commitment to other surrogate mothers.

On Tuesday, September 1, I traveled to Washington to appear before a Senate subcommittee on behalf of a group that had been created to provide moral and legal support for surrogates. Its goal was to unite several hundred women into a national support network and then press Congress for a law banning all commercial surrogate parenting contracts. "I think it's about time everyone in this country put an end to surrogate parenthood," I told the gathering of reporters and politicians who packed the press conference. "I can't do it by myself. I need everyone's help. Let's not have any more Saras."

Gena Corea, an organizer of the National Coalition Against Surrogacy, called surrogacy "the institutionalization of a new form of slavery" in which poor women were lured into lucrative-sounding deals by "unscrupulous breeder brokers." "Surrogacy violates human dignity and is unconscionable in a civilized society," she said.

Jeremy Rifkin, president of the Foundation on Economic Trends, explained that the Coalition would try to keep women from entering surrogate parenting contracts and to help surrogate mothers who were already pregnant to cope with the birth of their children.

"Childbearing, one of the most important of all human acts, is fast becoming a business," he told the group. He continued on this point:

> The surrogacy industry is advertising for services of financially stressed women all over America, soliciting them to bear children for clients who are willing to pay up to $25,000 for a baby. If this new industry is permitted to grow, within a decade thousands of poor women in this country and around the world will be used each year as "breeding stock" to gestate babies for those who can afford the service. . . . Attorneys, acting as commercial middlemen for clients, take advantage of these women and their dire circumstances. Once trapped, the women are unable to escape. . . . Some say that a surrogacy contract must be honored at all costs. They believe that commercial bonds should be given higher priority than maternal bonds, that money is more powerful than motherhood. It's strange that in this society we allow athletes, businessmen, and unions to break unjust or unfair contracts every day, but when it comes to the most important act of all, motherhood, we hold these women rigidly to their contracts.

Then Elizabeth Kane, the first surrogate mother to accept money and sign a contract, who, like so many of us, had originally believed that surrogacy was a wonderful way to help a childless couple, addressed the subcommittee:

> I gave birth to my son almost seven years ago and handed him, naked and cold, to a woman who was a stranger to me. Eight and one-half months earlier I had signed a

contract promising to transfer a live child to the wife of my baby's father. The day I signed that agreement, I was unknowingly stripped of all rights ever to see my son again. As a surrogate mother, I was only a means of transportation for this child to come into the world.

We have become a society that demands instant gratification, and now we are demanding instant babies by expecting healthy women to become our breeding stock. The fact that our society has accepted using breeders to create children for wealthy people frightens me.

It is by nature abnormal for any woman to psychologically disassociate herself from her child, yet we as a society are expecting women to sell a child that has not yet been conceived. . . . What is even more frightening is the fact that Americans can so coldheartedly criticize a woman for recognizing and admitting that she has fallen in love with her own child. . . . Taking a child away from its mother without her permission is the worst form of brutality and abuse I can imagine.

I willingly entered into a surrogate parenting agreement with the euphoric feeling of creating a family for a couple less fortunate than myself. While I was pregnant, I smugly answered all of the questions my children asked about the arrangement I had made for their brother. Today I can no longer explain to my children why I felt justified in exchanging their brother for a $10,000 check. By trying to create a family for a stranger, I created a dysfunctional family for myself. I want you to know that exchanging the emotional stability of a family for any amount of money is too great a price. . . . Surrogate parenting is an emotional minefield and I have become a statistic.

Today the child I've sold does not know I exist. My son's childhood was lost to me forever because of my rapid signature on a piece of paper before he even existed.

Moved by what I had heard, I, too, addressed the committee, gesturing toward the women sitting beside me:

I never stood a chance. Neither did Patty Foster, who watched what I was going through on television and read about it in the newspaper while she was pregnant with a son she could not bear to give away. She saw what happened to me and she felt she did not have a chance. Now her son is gone and she is fighting for him as hard as I am fighting for my daughter. Allejandra Munoz and Elizabeth Kane—none of us had a chance. It's not just Mary Beth Whitehead. It is all of us. We have started a mothers' support group to help each other. More and more of us are coming forward and saying that we are human beings. We are not baby-making machines.

Now, finally, through the National Coalition Against Surrogacy, I feel that I can do something to prevent other women from going through the suffering I have been through—am still going through. I can work with other mothers for laws banning this cruel business that sells human flesh and blood and pretends that nobody is hurt in the process.

When this all started for me, I thought surrogacy was a nice way of helping someone out. Now I know that surrogacy is wrong for our society. Now I know it is wrong to sell babies. And I know something else. It is also wrong to buy babies. I know it is wrong to use women as if they had no feelings. I know it is wrong to cause pain to the sisters and brothers of the babies who are sold through surrogacy contracts. It is wrong to hurt my daughter Tuesday. It is wrong to hurt my son Ryan. It is wrong that we mothers are not heard because we often lack wealth and education. I hope that this time, here in Congress, people will listen. The only crime we've committed was loving our babies too much.

I promised to continue my fight to help other women and to ban surrogacy in the United States just as it had been banned in Australia, Canada, Denmark, France, Germany, Great Britain, Ireland, Italy, Israel, Poland, and Sweden, all of which had roundly criticized Judge Sorkow's decision.

"The surrogate agreement is a violation of nature's law," I said. "I knew it from the moment my baby was born." Then, joining hands with Allejandra Munoz, I added, "I can't go to bed at night and just forget about this. A lot of people say, 'Let it die, leave it alone, go on with your life.' But this *is* my life."

# Chapter 19

# The New Jersey Supreme Court

When the law finally speaks, simple humanity requires it to say such contracts cannot be binding on biological mothers. To say otherwise would be a moral outrage of unconscionable dimensions.

> —Robert Maynard in the *Courier News*
> (Bridgewater, New Jersey),
> August 21, 1987

**T**wo weeks later we were back in court, the most progressive state supreme court in the nation. During the previous three months, Harold Cassidy's law firm had submitted, for its review, 250 pages of legal analysis, 2,500 pages of notes and appendices, and more than 7,000 pages of trial transcript.

The New Jersey Supreme Court has never hesitated to make new law or enter boldly into uncharted territory. In recent years it has issued rulings that prevented suburbs from zoning out the poor, and has affirmed the right of the terminally ill to be removed from life-support systems.

With thirty-two organizations filing friend-of-the-court briefs, most of which challenged Sorkow's ruling, the court was faced with three distinct questions: Should commercial surrogacy be banned? Should Sara remain in the Sterns' custody? Should my rights as a mother be terminated?

In a short opening statement, Harold Cassidy began to argue that although I had disobeyed Harvey Sorkow's order to turn my child over to the police, I had acted in compliance with a higher law, a law that says a mother should never abandon her baby.

"Mr. Cassidy," Chief Justice Robert Wilentz interrupted about three minutes into Harold's speech, "assume that the Supreme Court agrees with you and feels that the surrogate agreement should be void, you still have a child who has a natural father who seeks custody."

In what already seemed more like a working session than a formal court proceeding, Harold pointed out that under current state adoption laws, a mother has the right to change her mind after a child is born. He said that surrogate arrangements contradict accepted law, first by exploiting a woman who is in need of money and then by an improper separation of the child from its mother, solely in the interest of the father, even when we know that such separation puts the child at risk.

"We don't terminate the parental rights of fit mothers based on the exchange of money," he added with quiet intensity. "We have criminal statutes against this."

Harold also reminded the court that Sara would be with me today if Judge Sorkow hadn't authorized the police to take her from me without following the proper judicial procedure of a full hearing, during which Bill Stern would have had to prove me unfit. "Eighty percent of the facts being considered here today flow from an illegal order. There is a taint here. A fair hearing was never held," Harold said passionately. "In running from police who sought to seize her child, Mary Beth Whitehead acted like a mother who had been pressed to the wall and had been given no other recourse. It's like a beauty contest in which you punch the mother in the mouth, knock out all her teeth, and then criticize her for not having the prettiest smile." Then Harold paused. There were a hundred other points he could make, but he sensed that these were powerful enough to stand alone.

Next, Alan Karcher, Harold's co-counsel, argued that there was no male analog to pregnancy. Since a man finishes making his contribution at the moment of conception, Karcher called the leap from noncoital procreation to the right of exclusive male custody an invention of the lower court. "A man's right to custody," he insisted, "cannot be exercised without consideration for how it impacts on the competing interests of the mother."

With Rick and Tuesday beside me, I listened, amazed at the depth and philosophical scope of the questions the justices asked and the answers the attorneys provided.

When it was his turn to speak, Gary Skoloff urged the court to legalize surrogacy. "Infertile couples need your approval of the practice," he said. "I really hope you do rule on this issue. I think the state, the nation, the world is waiting for what this court decides. We are in new and uncharted territory."

"Mr. Skoloff," Justice Gary Stein said, clearing his throat, "do you think that the courts should sanction surrogacy contracts that call for an abortion if the fetus turns out to be of an unwanted sex? Or in cases where the wife of the man hiring the surrogate is not infertile but simply wants to avoid pregnancy?"

Skoloff looked uncomfortable. Then, from whatever answers crossed his mind, he seemed to choose the wrong one. "Such itty-bitty hypothetical questions are best left to the state legislature," he answered, forcing a smile. Not amused, Justice Robert Clifford accused Skoloff of ducking the question, then wondered out loud if the court should take any role at all.

When pressed by the court to explain how Judge Sorkow had ended my rights without finding that I was an unfit mother, as required by law, Skoloff asserted that Sorkow had in fact judged me to be an unfit mother.

Justice Clifford looked squarely at Skoloff. "I didn't find that," he said. "Perhaps I'm missing something. Can I press you to show me where in the decision that finding exists?"

Skoloff fumbled through several documents, then dropped the accusation, mumbling something about reading between the lines.

Chief Justice Wilentz intervened again, this time asking Skoloff whether he thought I should be granted visits with the baby if my parental rights were restored.

"That scenario would be the worst possible thing," Skoloff said.

"What does that mean?" the Chief Justice asked impatiently. "What are you suggesting? Did you ever hear of a case where a mother whose rights were not terminated had no rights?"

Skoloff shrugged. "Her only shot at happiness is termination," he answered.

Next, Lorraine Abraham stood before the judges. When asked if Sorkow's decision to terminate my rights was in conflict with the recommendation of two of her experts, her deepset eyes narrowed and her voice cracked. "Yes," she said. Then, while claiming that the discrepancy made the case even more complex, Lorraine Abraham urged that my rights not be terminated but that I be kept from seeing Sara for at least five years. She gave two reasons. The first was that I would exploit Sara in the media. The second was that I was too closely bonded to her.

Chief Justice Wilentz, who had consistently referred to me as the baby's mother while calling Bill Stern the sperm donor and Betsy the stepmother, sighed impatiently, then dismissed her. Although they did not indicate when they would make their decision, Harold Cassidy felt confident that, for the first time since this legal battle began, my side had finally been heard.

# Chapter 20

# A New Life

By these standards we are all unfit mothers. . . . We strongly urge legislators and jurists who deal with these matters to recognize that a mother need not be perfect to deserve her child.

> —From a statement signed by
> more than one hundred prominent
> women, released at the
> Bergen County Courthouse,
> March 12, 1987

**I** was still struggling with my feelings of loyalty to Rick, my love for Dean, and my concern about breaking up our family, when I discovered that I was pregnant. During a follow-up visit to my gynecologist for the second kidney infection, I mentioned that it had been almost two months since I had had my last period. I hadn't given it much thought since I had just stopped taking birth-control pills in an attempt to regulate my extremely irregular periods. That irregularity, along with a tipped uterus and severe endometriosis, which had led to an exploratory laparoscopy the previous December, had convinced me that I could never conceive again. Just the same, the doctor suggested a routine pregnancy test. As I stood there watching the liquid in the bottom of the vial turn blue, I felt myself growing weak. "Looks like you're going to have another baby, Mary," the nurse said, hugging me.

"Another baby," I whispered as I swayed on my feet, with a hundred emotions colliding. "A baby that no one can take away."

I was simultaneously elated and frightened. I was terribly worried about hurting Rick, and I didn't know how another pregnancy would affect my fight for Sara. I knew only one thing: If God was giving me another chance to be a mother, I was grateful beyond words. And no matter how people might react, I wasn't about to lose another baby.

With my hands trembling so much that I could hardly dial, I called Dean and told him the news. "That's wonderful, Mary," he said, laughing. "You and me and Baby make six. We will have to find a place right away that's big enough for us and all the kids."

As it turned out, I think that outsiders had a harder time accepting Dean and the pregnancy than my children did. The children knew all too well what I had been through, how the loss of Sara had changed me, and what the difficulties with the marriage were.

I told them what had happened as honestly and directly as I could. I said that whether they wanted to stay with their father or live with me was up to them. Tuesday and Ryan knew of Rick's long struggle with alcohol. While they loved and respected him, they understood how hard the drinking had been on all of us. Ultimately, both children decided that they wanted to stay with me. I remember Ryan saying he really still needed me to cook, iron his clothes, and make his bed. Tuesday had only two questions about Dean: "Does he drink, and does he want Sara?"

In that first flush of excitement and joy, I confided the news to one of the women who supervised my visits with Sara. To my dismay, as soon as I left, she called Lorraine Abraham and told her everything that I had said. Abraham in turn immediately wrote a letter to the Supreme Court, informing them that I was pregnant out of wedlock, and without additional facts or even confirmation, she now urged that they cut off all access to Sara until "the age of maturity." She added, "Regretfully, I must point out that Whitehead's action evidences the impulsivity, narcissism, and lack of mature judgment the mental health experts testified to at the trial."

That evening, while speaking at a Jewish Center in Bergen County, Abraham also told the audience that I was living in East Brunswick with a man named Dean. Since the audience happened to include Diane Diamond from the local CBS television news, the media descended. They brought their equipment and camera crews and camped for days outside our newly rented town house in East Brunswick.

We had just moved in. No one even knew we were there. Suddenly, we couldn't go out to walk the dogs. The kids were afraid to go to school. Neighbors were being stopped as they approached their apartments and asked if they thought I should be evicted. Some said yes. Their answers were appearing on network news.

The publisher who had originally planned to publish my book canceled the contract, saying that it was no longer a story they wanted to tell. And Gary Skoloff announced that the news underscored his contention that I was an unstable person with an unstable family unit. He added that it would reflect poorly on me if I had become pregnant when the Supreme Court ruling was imminent.

Dean was at work in New York when the news broke.

At his suggestion, Rick rushed over so that the kids and I wouldn't have to be home alone. When an aggressive reporter from the *New York Post* rang our bell, he looked as if he had seen a ghost and nearly fainted when Rick opened the door. Dozens of other reporters peered wide-eyed through ground-floor windows as Rick and I tacked up sheets in a futile effort to regain our privacy.

While I was still trying to decide how to handle the situation, Harold Cassidy issued a statement that said, "Nothing in Mrs. Whitehead's personal circumstances renders the surrogate contract enforceable. Her circumstances do not, nor could they ever, constitute grounds to terminate the mother's rights. They do not alter the fact that the baby, Sara-Melissa, should have as full a relationship as possible with both of her parents. The practice of surrogate parenting is no less harmful or indecent. The parents of Baby M are the litigants, but they are not the issue. None of this has changed."

That night I wondered once again if I should step away from Sara, but I still believed that she would never forgive me for walking out of her life, or denying her access to her siblings. The bottom line had not changed. I was still her mother.

By the next day I had gathered my own thoughts together. If I was going to be turned into a contemporary Hester Prynne and publicly shunned for my pregnancy, I might as well wear my scarlet letter proudly. With Dean standing beside me, I opened my front door and gave my own statement. I confirmed to the press that I was pregnant and that I wanted and would have my baby. I said that I loved Dean and that we would be married as soon as possible.

Rick filed for divorce in Middlesex County, New Jersey. Since I requested nothing in the way of support and we had agreed on joint custody, everything was finalized just two days after he filed.

Rick came to pick me up on the morning of our divorce. First I ironed his shirt for court, then we faced the press together. Making light of a difficult situation, we smiled as the cameras clicked. Since the terms had already been decided, we signed the papers as quickly as possible and then went out to breakfast. The divorce was so traumatic that we were still trying to handle it by pretending that nothing important had happened.

Two weeks after the divorce was finalized, Dean and I were married in a small, private, Saturday-morning ceremony at the home of Peggy and Alan Karcher's daughter, Ellen. The Karchers had become like family to me. So had my bridesmaid, Dr. Michelle Harrison, the psychiatrist and obstetrician from Boston, who had been among that first group of feminists who rallied to my defense. Whenever things were particularly difficult, I would call Michelle and tell her what was happening. She was a professional, and her reassurance had a way of making me feel sane again.

She was especially important on those days when the prisonlike visits with Sara became so hard and painful that I felt I couldn't return. Michelle would always help me to understand that I had to go back because Sara needed to see me. She always seemed able to help me find that final measure of strength that I didn't think I had.

Now, as Dean and I stood surrounded by my children, Michelle Harrison, Peggy Karcher, Alison Ward, and other close friends, with our parents beside us, we smiled as photographers snapped our picture.

For weeks, the reporters had been calling City Hall in East Brunswick to find out when the wedding would be. I knew that the press would be there anyhow, so when *The*

*Star* approached us and offered to actually pay us for the photographs, I agreed. I didn't like doing it, but I still had over $10,000 in bills from my hospitalization in Florida. I also had more legal bills for the case than I could begin to put a price tag on. I had given all the proceeds from the sale of our house to Rick so that he could start a business. I had also waived all of my child support or alimony because I knew Rick would always do whatever he could for his children. Nevertheless, I was penniless. Dean and I needed to set up a new household, and despite what people thought about my wealthy accountant, Dean was young, just starting his career, and very short of money.

Just the same, I was more at peace than I could ever remember being. I was more mature now and far more ready to commit myself than I had been when I married Rick at the age of sixteen.

"It's the happiest day of my life," Dean said after the judge pronounced us man and wife.

"Mine too, Dean," I answered, laughing. "Mine too."

# Chapter 21

# Justice

What [the Supreme Court] really did was rule that a human soul was more important than a contract, that Judge Sorkow's philosophy that a deal is a deal is wrong when the deal involves the selling of a human being. Seven to zero wrong.

—A. M. Rosenthal in *The New York Times*, February 5, 1988

**O**n February 2, 1988, Harold Cassidy finally received the call that we had all been waiting for since September. The Supreme Court decision was going to be released the next morning.

Slowly, over the long months of waiting, I had given up most of the dream of regaining custody of Sara. I knew that once she'd lived a year and a half with the Sterns, no court in the land would uproot her again. And while I still longed to have her come home forever, I also understood that too much time had passed for that to happen without hurting her. The last thing I ever wanted to do was cause Sara more pain by uprooting and confusing her again. By this time I had also accepted the fact that the Sterns loved her and would do everything they could for her.

I think I was as prepared as I ever could be to let go of the dream that my daughter was coming home to stay. And yet, as we gathered at the Molly Pitcher Inn for a hastily called press conference, and everyone around me hugged and congratulated me, I felt like a soldier who had won a battle but lost the war. Except for the issue of custody, the Supreme Court had overturned every aspect of Judge Harvey Sorkow's decision. The ruling restored my parental rights and vacated Betsy's adoption. It announced that I would have some kind of visitation, to be decided by a lower court, but not by Judge Harvey Sorkow. And it declared commercial surrogacy illegal.

I stood before the press, surrounded by adoption groups and anti-surrogacy groups. It was a bittersweet half-victory, won at deep personal cost. Despite all my preparation, it was still difficult to let go of custody. With Rick on one side of me and Harold on the other, I began to read my prepared speech. I thanked my children, my parents, and Rick. Then, suddenly, I was crying. There were no words to adequately thank my family, especially Rick, for all he had gone through and lost. He touched my hand. As usual, Rick understood without being told.

"I'm glad that the months of uncertainty are finally over," I said, borrowing a Kleenex and collecting myself. "This long, difficult struggle has changed all of our lives. I want to thank the justices of the Supreme Court for overturning Judge Sorkow's decision and for allowing me to continue to see my daughter while they considered the facts of the case. Her smile when we visited once a week and her tears when we parted always gave me the strength to carry on. I did not begin this as a public crusade, but I am gratified to see surrogacy discredited and delighted to know that my relationship with my daughter will be allowed to continue for the rest of our lives." Then I reminded the press that, as I had told them almost a year ago, there could never be a "court-appointed termination of my love for Sara."

Rick also read a prepared speech telling the crowd how happy he was for me and for the baby. Public speaking was hard for him, but he wanted people to know that he was still behind me. "I'm here today," Rick began with his hands trembling, "simply to say that I'm happy for Mary and for Sara. I was with Mary when Sara was born; I helped Mary when she decided that she could not go through with the surrogacy agreement; I was involved throughout the trial. I'm happy that the courts of New Jersey have recognized that Mary had a right to reject the surrogacy agreement. I'm especially happy that, as Sara grows up, Mary will be a part of her life. I truly believe that Sara will be the better for it."

Harold was buoyant. The Supreme Court's opinion had echoed his argument. "We accomplished everything we hoped to accomplish with this appeal," he said. "I think the opinion is the death knell for commercial surrogacy. I also think it is a marvelous victory for all women who seek to play a role in the raising of their children."

The Sterns, on the other hand, made it known through Gary Skoloff that they were "troubled by the order regarding visitation . . . perplexed by the complexity of the opinion, and stunned by the repudiation of Judge Sorkow's ruling."

"It's a bad turn for surrogacy," Gary Skoloff acknowledged at his own press conference. "Without judicial sanction, it will now be necessary for the legislature to write new laws. But surrogacy is just the kind of issue politicians would rather leave to the courts. It's such a hot potato, nobody wants to mess with it. Besides," he concluded, "without payment there will be no surrogates or very few."

All around the country, experts were concurring. While many believed that the decision was not legally binding beyond the state's borders, its impact could still destroy the commercial practice of surrogate motherhood in the United States. Because of the lack of legal precedent on the subject, state courts and legislatures would probably turn to this decision for guidance as they grappled with whether to outlaw commercial surrogacy or to regulate it in their own states. Even Noel Keane acknowledged that other states and other judges would seriously review this decision.

Andrew Kimbrell, an attorney for the National Coalition Against Surrogacy, said, "There should be no hesitation by state legislatures or Congress to ban commercial surrogacy. The court ruling is historic. It will mark the beginning of the end of commercialized childbirth in this country."

Kimbrell was right. Four months later, in June of 1988, state legislators all over the country were moving to impose regulations, outright bans, and even prison terms.

James J. Blanchard, Governor of Noel Keane's home state of Michigan, passed the nation's first law making it a felony to arrange a surrogate mother contract for money. The law, which went into effect on September 1, 1988, provided a $50,000 fine and five years in prison for acting as a surrogate broker.

In Florida, Governor Bob Martinez signed similar felony legislation. Louisiana, Nebraska, Indiana, and Kentucky also enacted legislation prohibiting enforcement of surrogate contracts, and a California measure was expected.

But, back in February, the lawyers continued to debate, and I continued to watch with an amazed mixture of gratitude and cynicism as public opinion shifted. Suddenly, ABC's "World News Tonight" named Harold Cassidy the "Person of the Week." Ted Koppel asked him to appear on "Nightline" again, this time without Gary Skoloff. And throughout the United States, press accounts were honoring me for my tenacity and applauding the anticipated demise of surrogacy.

A. M. Rosenthal of *The New York Times* praised the judges for striking down Judge Sorkow's attempt to deny my existence. "Nobody has the right to separate mother and child forever," he wrote. "It was an act of judicial anger and vindictiveness to do so in the first place."

Syndicated columnist Murray Kempton added, "She had put before these judges a copy book not altogether immaculate and they have looked behind its blotchings and seen her essential honor plain."

Columnist Claude Lewis said, "The well-balanced decision makes me want to stand up and cheer."

Even some of my own family, who had been so uncomfortable about my struggle that they had stopped calling and simply withdrew, now seemed to rethink their reactions. A letter arrived from my sister Beverly, whom I had not seen or heard from since the day I took Sara home from the Sterns' house, in which she said, "The real reason I'm writing is to tell you how sorry I am for not being there when you really needed me." She said she had regretted not being by my side "ever since this nightmare began." "You see," she continued, "I know better than anybody what it's like to be without a child but I would never take one away from its mother." My sister ended the letter by expressing her hope that the entire family could get together as a family once again.

I think that letter meant more to me than any other I

have ever received. Beverly and I had always been close, and I had missed her deeply.

It wasn't until several days later, after I had partially absorbed the sudden shift in so many people's reactions, that I sat down alone late at night in my kitchen and tried to understand exactly what all of this would mean for Sara and for me. I was still working on exchanging the illusion that she would soon be home to stay for the reality that I would always be a part of her life, albeit a limited part. As I sat there thinking and rethinking the last two years and trying to come to terms with the losses and the victories, I took out my copy of the ninety-five-page opinion, so eloquently written by Chief Justice Robert Wilentz. In the hours that followed, I began to understand how pro- foundly the court had perceived both my suffering and the Sterns'. Sadly I realized that some people would remember only the picture the Sterns had painted, a portrait resketched in acid by an ABC-TV miniseries about the case, written and filmed before the Supreme Court reversal, with an eye to justifying Sorkow's termination.

The Supreme Court couldn't totally erase that dis- torted image, but they made it far easier to bear. With the bombs of public opinion falling all around them, these seven judges had remained invincible. With clear and riveted vision, they had culled through thousands and thousands of pages of court records. More important, they had seen and encompassed not only my suffering, but Bill's and Betsy's and Rick's as well. They had looked beyond all of our private and public images and beyond our objective and subjective responses. They had mea- sured all of our errors and all of our transgressions and then they had written:

> It seems to us that given her predicament, Mrs. Whitehead was rather harshly judged—both by the trial court and by

some of the experts. She was guilty of a breach of contract and indeed, she did break a very important promise, but we think it is expecting something well beyond normal human capabilities to suggest that this mother should have parted with her newly born infant without a struggle. Other than survival, what stronger force is there? We do not know of, and cannot conceive of, any other case where a perfectly fit mother was expected to surrender her newly born infant, perhaps forever, and was then told she was a bad mother because she did not. We know of no authority suggesting that the moral quality of her act in these circumstances should be judged by referring to a contract made before she became pregnant. We do not countenance, and would never countenance, violating a court order as Mrs. Whitehead did, even a court order that is wrong. But her resistance to an order that she surrender her infant, possibly forever, merits a measure of understanding. We do not find it so clear that her efforts to keep her infant, when measured against the Sterns' efforts to take her away, make one, rather than the other, the wrongdoer. The Sterns suffered, but so did she. And if we go beyond suffering to an evaluation of the human stakes involved in the struggle, how much weight should be given to her nine months of pregnancy, the labor of childbirth, the risk to her life, compared to the payment of money, the anticipation of the child and the donation of sperm.

The justices of the Supreme Court breathed new life into the concept of justice. They realized that we had all been driven by passions that we could no longer control. They did not need to vilify one person in order to justify another. They did not need to complete the character assassination that Judge Sorkow and the Sterns had begun. Instead, they tried to dispel the damage by replacing the distortions with the truth:

There has emerged a portrait of Mrs. Whitehead exposing her children to the media, engaging in negotiations to sell a book, granting interviews that seemed helpful to her, whether hurtful to Baby M or not, that suggests a selfish, grasping woman, ready to sacrifice the interest of Baby M and her other children for fame and wealth. That portrait is a half-truth, for while it may accurately reflect what ultimately occurred, its implication, that this is what Mary Beth Whitehead wanted, is totally inaccurate, at least insofar as the record before us is concerned. There is not one word in that record to support a claim that had she been allowed to continue her possession of her newly born infant, Mrs. Whitehead would have ever been heard of again; not one word in the record suggests that her change of mind and her subsequent fight for her child was motivated by anything other than love—whatever complex, underlying psychological motivations may have existed.

The Supreme Court also looked at the difference in our educational backgrounds:

We have a further concern regarding the trial court's emphasis on the Sterns' interest in Melissa's education as compared to the Whiteheads'. That this difference is a legitimate factor to be considered, we have no doubt. But it should not be overlooked that a best-interest test is designed to create not a new member of the intelligentsia but rather a well-integrated person who might reasonably be expected to be happy with life. . . . Stability, love, family happiness, tolerance, and ultimately the support of independence, all rank much higher in predicting future happiness than the likelihood of a college education.

Most important of all, they ruled that Judge Sorkow's May 5 *ex parte* order was wrong and illegal. They clearly stated that Sara should never have been taken from my custody by police, without a prior hearing. From this point forward, any application for custody by a natural father in a surrogacy dispute will require proof of unfitness or danger to the child before the child is taken.

In some ways, my partial victory was hard to bear. The contract that I had signed was now illegal and unenforceable, and yet it *had* been enforced. Surrogate parenting was indeed baby-selling. I had never accepted any money. The Sterns' $10,000 had stayed in the court's escrow account and had ultimately been returned to them. Still, my child had been bought by expensive legal tactics.

In response to Gary Skoloff's argument that the Sterns were buying services, not a baby, the justices wrote:

> We need note only that they would pay nothing in the event the child died before the fourth month of pregnancy, and only $1,000 if the child were stillborn, even though the "services" had been fully rendered. . . . This is the sale of a child, or, at the very least, the sale of the mother's right to her child, the only mitigating factor being that one of the purchasers is the father. Almost every evil that promoted the prohibition of the payment of money in connection with adoption exists here. . . . Whatever idealism may have motivated any of the participants, the profit motive predominates, permeates and ultimately governs the transaction. . . . There are, in a civilized society, some things that money cannot buy. . . . The long-term effects of surrogacy contracts are not known, but feared—the impact on the child who learns her life was bought. . . ; the impact on the natural mother as the full weight of her isolation is felt along with the full reality of the sale of her body and her child; the impact on the natural father and the adoptive mother once they realize the consequences of their conduct. . . . The Sterns knew almost from the very

day that they took Baby M that their rights were being challenged by the natural mother. . . . There is simply no basis . . . to warrant termination of Mrs. Whitehead's parental rights. We therefore conclude that the natural mother is entitled to retain her rights as a mother.

Before turning the matter of visitation over to the lower courts, they quietly but explicitly instructed the judge to recall that I was not to be punished "one iota" for signing the surrogacy contract, that it was desirable for a child to have contact with both parents, and that the decision was to be reached within ninety days.

# Chapter 22

# The Wisdom of
# a Solomon

At a stroke, New Jersey's Supreme Court brought clarity and
justice to the Baby M case, which so tormented the nation.

—Editorial in *The New York Times*,
February 4, 1988

**S**uperior Court Judge Bir-
ger Sween had been assigned to the case by County
Assignment Judge Peter Ciolino. The slender, gracious,
fifty-eight-year-old ordained deacon and father of three
had also served on the Bergen County ethics committee
and the county welfare board. He seemed entirely at ease
as he sat surrounded by five murals depicting great moments in the development of law, with the word "Peace"
on one side of him and "Justice" on the other.

"Are there any facts in dispute?" he inquired as soon
as the proceeding began. When neither side could produce any, Bill Stern was called to the stand. At first Sween
listened politely as Gary Skoloff asked questions about the
baby's routine. But he sighed impatiently when Skoloff
seemed ready to go on indefinitely with minute details.

"Breakfast is not of interest to the court," Sween finally said as Bill began to describe Sara leading him to the refrigerator and selecting peanut butter and jelly each morning at six o'clock.

"I was just trying to give the court a picture," Skoloff answered defensively.

Sween nodded. "Move on to something else," he said.

Perhaps sensing that he was already in trouble, Skoloff changed the subject. "How do you think Mary Beth feels about you?" he asked.

Instantly, Bill Stern tensed. "She hates my guts. She holds me responsible for her divorce and all the upheaval to her children," he blurted out, his face distorted by emotions.

Suddenly it became obvious that the Supreme Court's reversal and vindication of me had had no impact on Bill Stern. He was still trying to use the old tactic of unsubstantiated assaults that had worked in Judge Sorkow's courtroom. "I have no reason to believe that Mary Beth is sincere about anything," he said. "I don't want to see Melissa undermined and destroyed by Mary Beth. Mary Beth would distort her view and undermine her trust in Betsy and me. I can't believe anything she says. . . . One thing I've learned is that Mary Beth lies. How am I supposed to deal with her if I can't trust her?"

"Mr. Stern," the judge interrupted, apparently wanting to end the unsupportable claims and accusations and bring the discussion back to practical issues. "You're Jewish, your wife is Protestant, and I believe from the record that Mary Beth Whitehead is Catholic."

"I'm not practicing," Bill Stern replied.

"Do you observe the holidays?" the judge asked.

Bill nodded and drew in his breath. "The other night

I drove past a temple and I wanted to take her in," he said; then, as if the memory had suddenly recalled old pain and guilt, his voice broke and tears streamed down his face. "I know she can't be Jewish," he sobbed, "but I want Melissa to know about her Jewish heritage."

"Have you discussed your religious plans with your wife?" the judge asked gently.

"Our plans are to join the Unitarian Church," Bill said, taking a sip of water and struggling to regain some measure of composure. "We decorate the house on Christmas Eve. On Easter Sunday we go to church together."

During the trial, much had been made of the fact that Bill Stern's relatives had been killed in the Holocaust. The court-appointed experts had argued that Bill felt bereft of family and saw surrogacy as a way to "enable him to have a biological link to another person," something he had lost at the time of his mother's death.

The press had often treated the subject as if Bill, rather than his parents, had survived the Holocaust. But the fact was that Bill Stern was born after World War II and grew up in the United States. Also, according to Dr. Greif's report, while Bill loved and got along with his father, who died when he was twelve, he had a "conflictual relationship" with his mother and often complained that she "wouldn't let go." Once Bill moved away to go to graduate school in Michigan, he visited her only twice a year. While it is true that Bill had me artificially inseminated only thirteen months after his mother's death, it is also true that he knew that according to Jewish law, a child is only Jewish if its mother is Jewish.

Now, as Bill spoke with so much emotion, I couldn't help wondering why a nonpracticing, German-born Jew, who apparently had such strong religious feelings, was attending services at a Presbyterian church and planning to raise his daughter as a Unitarian. Nor could I understand why he and Betsy received counseling for nine months with a Presbyterian pastoral counselor. Most of all, I was puzzled by the fact that he had chosen a Protestant woman to be his wife, and an Irish Catholic of German descent to be the mother of his child.

"So you'd like her to be with you on Jewish holidays and on Christian holidays, too," the judge said, interpreting Bill's obvious anguish.

"Yes," Bill said.

"Mary Beth is a Catholic. Do you," the judge asked, "have any objection to the baby going to church?"

"We all believe in God," Bill said, clearing his throat. "We practice in different ways. I have no objection to Melissa going to church."

Even though Bill still had custody of our daughter, in some ways I was beginning to feel as if our roles had been reversed. He was so emotionally volatile, so ready to lash out and at the same time so close to tears, that he seemed as near to breaking under the strain as I had ever been. I now felt myself calm and controlled by comparison. I wanted to heal our relationship for the sake of our baby, but he was still not ready. Likening me to a baby-sitter named Ann, whom the baby was fond of but with whom she had an insignificant relationship, Bill asked for an end to all visitation.

Even after he finally stepped down from the witness stand, Betsy continued with the same line of argument. "If visitation were stopped tomorrow, I don't think Melissa would know the difference," she said.

She, too, compared me to the baby-sitter. "I've watched Ann and Mary Beth interact many times," she said, inadvertently confusing my name with Melissa's. "I think we should wait until adolescence. I know Mary Beth will do anything, say anything to get what she wants. She's very manipulative." Then, with tightened lips and trembling hands, she added, "I don't have any respect for her. I'd never choose her as a friend. We don't share any common values. We are poles apart. I know she'll undermine Bill and me as custodial parents."

"Talk about undermining," Joel Siegal, the Newark attorney acting as counsel to Harold Cassidy's firm, whispered as he patted my shoulder and walked toward the witness stand for his cross-examination. "Dr. Stern, do you recognize that Mary Beth also has rights?" he asked.

"Yes," Betsy answered. "The Supreme Court has said that."

"Has it ever occurred to you," Siegal pressed, "that the best solution might be to face it now?"

"I've considered all possibilities," Betsy said, "but I feel that there must be a hiatus. Quite frankly, Mr. Siegal, we don't trust Mary Beth."

"Dr. Stern," Siegal responded patiently, "if Melissa had a good relationship with you, with Mary Beth, and with her father, wouldn't that be the best result?"

Betsy Stern shook her head. With an attempt at composure that failed to hide her animosity, she said, "I don't think that's possible. I don't trust Mary Beth. I know she lies."

"Dr. Stern, you called Mary Beth a liar. Your husband called Mary Beth a liar. Your husband said he sees no disadvantage whatever in terminating visitation. Isn't your husband a liar when he says that? You say you want her to be like all the other kids. You're afraid she'll feel like a freak. Wouldn't Melissa be more like every other kid on the block if she had visitation, and if she knew who both of her natural parents really were?"

"I don't know how the court sees me," Betsy answered. Then she shut her eyes, as if trying to blot out the reality. "In the eyes of the law, I don't know who I am . . . the stepmother, the custodial parent. But in my heart of hearts, to precious little Melissa, I know I'm her mother." Then, with her face flushed and her mouth set firmly, she added, "In my heart of hearts, I can't understand how visitation at this time in Melissa's little life will be of any benefit to her."

Joel Siegal started to ask another question, but the judge shook his head. He looked weary. We all did. Bill and Betsy Stern's day in court was over.

Even now, people ask me how I managed to remain calm in the face of so much personal assault. I think some of it was the passage of time and the growing acceptance of loss. Another part of it was the peace I had found in my new marriage and the gentle stirring of life within me again. I had been blessed with another chance to experience the joy and pain of motherhood. And although no one could ever replace Sara, I was grateful beyond words to have the opportunity to do it the right way this time.

I had also found consolation and comfort in the opinion of the seven justices of the Supreme Court. They had looked at the issues closely and without bias, and they had given me back a measure of self-respect, which the Sterns could never again take away, no matter what they said, or how many stones they threw. They could no longer break my spirit because *I* knew who I was.

In an effort to be open and direct, Joel Siegal began by asking me a series of questions about my divorce and remarriage. I explained that after our marriage of fourteen years, Rick had remained close to my family and was currently living in Florida with one of my brothers. I said that he occasionally stayed overnight at our town house, and that Dean and Rick sometimes went bowling together. "Their relationship is very good," I explained. "There is no animosity."

"You mean nobody hates anybody's guts?" Siegal asked, deliberately using Bill Stern's phrase.

"No," I answered, glancing at Harold's associate, Bob Ruggieri, who smiled supportively. "We all get along."

"What is the time you've spent with Melissa?" Siegal inquired.

"Not enough," I said. The judge smiled. "I love her very much," I continued calmly, "and I know she loves me. There is something very special between us. I heard yesterday that I was no different to her than a baby-sitter. I know that's not true. If you could see her there with me and how differently she reacts to me than to the other people in the room, you would know it too. As soon as she sees me, she hugs me for the first five minutes. She cries when it's time to leave."

Then Joel Siegal turned toward me and directly confronted another difficult subject—the baby's name. He pointed out that the Sterns complained that I still called her Sara.

"I did refer to her as Sara," I said. "That was the name on her birth certificate. That is the name I had her baptized with. Giving up the name is very difficult. Sometimes I still call her Sara, but I do my best not to do it when I'm with her, simply because I don't want to confuse her. She is my child, whatever her name is."

I also acknowledged that I had referred to Bill as a sperm donor, and in a sense, during the nine months of my pregnancy and the period immediately following the baby's birth, that was what I felt. I pointed out that the Supreme Court had also consistently referred to him as "the donor." I said that I no longer thought of him as simply a sperm donor and always called him "Daddy" when speaking to our daughter. "I'm willing to meet them more than halfway," I added.

"And how do you feel about having visitation but not custody?"

"I let go of my dream of having custody a long time ago," I answered quietly. "I just want to love her. I want to be her mother. I don't want to undermine the Sterns in any way. That would only hurt her."

"Mary Beth, how do you feel about a hiatus?" Siegal asked as he turned to face the judge.

"Life is too short," I answered. "There's a chance I would never know her or that Ryan or Tuesday would never know her. That would not be good for the Sterns either. She would resent them."

"Are you willing to cooperate with the Sterns in regard to transportation?"

"I'll make any sacrifice that has to be made in order to see my daughter."

"Would you like to see an end to the litigation?"

"Yes," I said. "I pray for that every day."

Judge Sween smiled warmly, then chuckled, when Julia Wiggins, a heavyset, middle-aged black woman who had supervised my visits with the baby, testified that I called her "oodee-bop," a pet name, during visits.

"And what does the baby call her?" Gary Skoloff's co-counsel, Frank Donahue, responded, unamused.

"Mama," Mrs. Wiggins answered matter-of-factly.

The courtroom stirred. This was a new piece of information that clearly surprised people.

"And has she kissed Mary Beth?" Donahue asked accusingly.

"Yes," Mrs. Wiggins said, nodding.

"And does Mary Beth kiss her?" he continued, as if he were unearthing a crime.

"Yes," she said, looking bewildered. Then, with a simplicity that added to her power as a witness, she added, "To me, it was just a normal mother-child relationship."

Joel Siegal held up a notebook and flipped through the pages. "According to the log you kept, the visitations you supervised began in October of 1986. On twenty-eight occasions, the only comment you made was 'visit went well' or 'visit went very well.' What did that mean?"

"It meant that everything went well. It meant that Mrs. Whitehead was good with the child and the child was good with her. Like I said, to me, it's just a normal mother-child relationship."

"Did Mary Beth bring changes of clothing?" Siegal asked, referring to the fact that, although it annoyed the Sterns, I tried to buy Sara one new outfit a month. I did it because I enjoyed seeing her in pretty things and because helping to take care of her, in whatever way I could, made me feel more like her mother. Once, when she was just starting to walk and I thought she needed shoes, I traced the outline of her feet on a piece of paper and took it to a shoe store. I sent a pair of Buster Brown walking shoes home with her. But as was the case with so many of the outfits, I never saw them again.

"Did she bring the baby new clothing?" Siegal asked again.

"Yes," Julia Wiggins answered.

"How often?"

"Many times," Julia Wiggins said, looking at me and nodding.

In addition to Julia Wiggins, two experts testified. Lee Salk, who still had not met me or observed me with the baby, recommended no contact until the child was twelve years old.

Harold Koplowitz, a psychiatrist who testified on my behalf and who conducted extensive interviews with me and observed me for two hours through a one-way mirror as I interacted with the baby, suggested a gradually increasing schedule of unsupervised visitation.

"Mary Beth spends less time with Melissa than the sitter does," Frank Donahue reminded Koplowitz. "So don't you think that if the visits were terminated, she'd have a brief sense of loss and then just get over it?"

"No," Koplowitz answered, "I don't. To begin with, she calls Mary Beth 'Mama,' and that means something special to her."

"You think she knows Mary Beth is her mother?" Donahue asked incredulously.

"I think 'Mama' represents someone special," Koplowitz said in response, "someone who is loving and nice."

"But," Donahue continued as if he thought he finally had an edge, "what makes these two hours different from time with anyone else?"

Before answering, Koplowitz hesitated. He looked at Bill Stern and then at me. "They do share a history, Mr. Donahue," he said. "This is the mother. She nursed the child, she was the primary caretaker. You know," he said, fixing his eyes directly on Betsy Stern, "it would be very hard for anyone to stay in a small room for two hours with a two-year-old. But Mary Beth did it. She more than did it. Somehow she managed to meet every one of that child's needs. Those two hours were very intense, very loving. Mary Beth created a world within that room, a very appropriate, warm, loving world. There were coloring books, and beads, and toys, and picture books. When the baby wanted lotion, Mary Beth put lotion on her. She fixed her hair. She had a photo album. The baby looked at the pictures, and she was able to identify Tuesday, Ryan, and Grandma and Grandpa. About a half hour into it, she climbed onto Mary Beth's lap. She hugged her and kissed her and called her mama. She was completely happy, completely at home, completely relaxed."

"Now it *is* possible, Mr. Donahue," Koplowitz added, pausing for emphasis, "that Mary Beth Whitehead was putting her best foot forward because she knew I was watching. But I don't think that little Melissa Stern was putting on a show for me."

Judge Sween chuckled, Bill Stern squirmed uncomfortably, and Betsy sat frozen, with only her eyes on fire.

In his closing argument, Donahue continued the old-line tactics. He was still calling me a liar and asserting that if I really loved my daughter, I'd give her up, when Judge Sween finally and mercifully tapped his pencil.

One week later, on April 7, 1988, without Judge Sorkow's fanfare or anger, and without the Supreme Court's philosophical overview, Judge Birger Sween issued his ruling on visitation. It had a simplicity and quiet eloquence all its own:

> The court finds that Melissa's best interests will be served by unsupervised, uninterrupted, liberal visitation with her mother. . . . Melissa is a resilient child who is no less capable than thousands of children of broken marriages who successfully adjust to complex family relationships when their parents remarry. . . . William and Elizabeth Stern must accept and understand that Melissa will develop a different and special relationship with her mother, stepfather, siblings, and extended family, and that these

relationships need not diminish their parent-child relationship with Melissa.

Ironically, my separation and divorce from Rick and subsequent marriage to Dean actually helped me. The Judge wrote that "at the time of the original order for supervised visitation, family and financial crises engulfed her marriage, and she was under the stress of having lost custody of her newborn baby. Since that time her marital problems have been resolved through divorce, and she has attained family stability with her new husband."

The ten-thirty to four-thirty weekly visits were to start immediately. They were to be increased by one day, on alternate weeks, beginning in September of 1988. In order to smooth the transition for the baby, Bill and I were to meet at the Conklin Center for the first three visits and he was to hand her directly to me. The baby would spend alternate holidays with me and, starting in April of 1989, she would stay with me overnight, every other week. She would also spend two weeks with me in the summer.

"This is no longer a termination of parental rights or adoption case," Judge Sween wrote at one point in his decision. "It no longer matters how Melissa was conceived. She and her mother have the right to develop their own special relationship."

# Chapter 23

# The Homecoming

It has long been obvious that "surrogate" motherhood has a terrible potential for causing pain. The New Jersey Supreme Court's wise decision may finally relieve some agony for Mrs. Whitehead-Gould and the Sterns. As important, it reinforces sound values for all who aspire to parenthood.

—Editorial in *The New York Times*, February 4, 1988

**B**ill Stern rubbed his eyes with his hand, and glanced around the Conklin Center as if he was looking for someone to help him. He appeared troubled and unable to comprehend that this was actually happening. Then, silently, he handed our daughter to me.

"Wave bye-bye to Da-da, Melissa. Throw Da-da a kiss," I said, realizing how hard it must have been and trying to make it easier for him. I wanted to tell him that I knew what he was going through, and still remembered my own desperation when I handed her over to him. In spite of all that had happened, he was still my child's father and I wanted to reach out to him and be his friend.

"Do you have a car seat?" he asked quietly.

"Yes," I answered, "I do."

For a moment, Bill looked at me as if he, too, wanted to say something, but couldn't. His lower lip quivered. "Don't feed her too many cookies," he whispered hoarsely as he turned away.

By this time the baby had wiggled out of my arms and had begun tugging at my hand and leading me back to the shabby room that had served as our meeting place for so many months.

"Not today, honey," I said, shaking my head and smiling. Then it occurred to me that perhaps she would be frightened by a change in our routine. After all, that tiny room, with its peeling paint and guarded doorway, had been the only world we'd shared since she was four months old. "Today is a very special day," I said as I picked her up and carried her past reporters, photographers, and a guard with a loaded gun on his hip. Instinctively, I hesitated, half expecting the guard to stop me. I smiled tentatively at him. He smiled back and waved.

"Good-bye, Mary Beth, and good luck to you," he said.

I felt my eyes fill up with tears. "Come on, sweetheart," I whispered, hugging her tightly. "We're going home now. We're finally going home."

She looked directly into my eyes, and then she smiled at me as if she understood. After a moment, she put her small hand in mine and squeezed it tightly. "Home, Mama, home," she said softly.